# Shrubs & Trees

THE BEST OF
FINE GARDENING

# Shrubs & Trees

The Taunton Press

Cover photo: Skip Kremer

Back-cover photos: left, Allen Rokach;
top right, Michael Shoup, Jr.; bottom right, Mark Kane

**Taunton**
BOOKS & VIDEOS

*for fellow enthusiasts*

© 1993 by The Taunton Press, Inc.
All rights reserved.

First printing: July 1993
Printed in the United States of America

A FINE GARDENING Book

FINE GARDENING® is a trademark of The Taunton Press, Inc.,
registered in the U.S. Patent and Trademark Office.

The Taunton Press
63 South Main Street
Box 5506
Newtown, CT 06470-5506

Library of Congress Cataloging-in-Publication Data

The Best of fine gardening. Shrubs & trees.
    p.  cm.
    Articles originally published in Fine gardening magazine.
    "A Fine gardening book"—T.p. verso.
    Includes index.
    ISBN 1-56158-055-4
    1. Ornamental shrubs. 2. Ornamental trees. I. Fine gardening.
SB435.B48  1993                           93-3134
635.9'76—dc20                           CIP

# Contents

**Introduction** . . . . . . . . . . . . . . . . . . . . . . . . . 7

**Lilacs** . . . . . . . . . . . . . . . . . . . . . . . . . . . . . . . 8
*Fragrant blooms from long-lived shrubs*

**Tree Peonies** . . . . . . . . . . . . . . . . . . . . . . 12
*Breathtaking blossoms on long-lived shrubs*

**Viburnums** . . . . . . . . . . . . . . . . . . . . . . . . 17
*Handsome foliage, white flowers and bright berries grace
a durable shrub*

**Buckeyes** . . . . . . . . . . . . . . . . . . . . . . . . . . 22
*These easy-care shrubs deserve wider attention*

**In Praise of Pieris** . . . . . . . . . . . . . . . . . . 26
*A spring-flowering evergreen shrub for shade*

**Old Roses for the Small Garden** . . . . . 30
*A wealth of blooms from tough, hardy shrubs*

**Old Roses** . . . . . . . . . . . . . . . . . . . . . . . . . 36
*Undemanding ornamentals for the landscape*

**Miniature Roses** . . . . . . . . . . . . . . . . . . . 42
*Freed from pots, they're versatile roses for the garden*

**Rosa Rubrifolia** . . . . . . . . . . . . . . . . . . . . 48
*Grow this rose for its multicolored foliage*

**Hardy Magnolias** . . . . . . . . . . . . . . . . . . 50
*Brilliant blossoms for colder climes*

**Outstanding Crabapples** . . . . . . . . . . . . 56
*How to make the right choice for your landscape*

**Redbuds** . . . . . . . . . . . . . . . . . . . . . . . . . . . 61
*Clouds of spring color from small ornamental trees*

**Fringe Trees** . . . . . . . . . . . . . . . . . . . . . . . 66
*Small beauties yield a cloud of bloom*

**Weeping Trees** . . . . . . . . . . . . . . . . . . . . . 68
*Make secret rooms of green*

**Hollies** . . . . . . . . . . . . . . . . . . . . . . . . . . . . 74
*Deck the garden with these versatile, evergreen shrubs
and trees*

**The Mighty Oaks** . . . . . . . . . . . . . . . . . . 80
*Tough trees to beautify your landscape*

**Eastern Red Cedar** . . . . . . . . . . . . . . . . . 85
*An appreciation of an overlooked tree*

**Dwarf Conifers** . . . . . . . . . . . . . . . . . . . . 89
*Compact evergreens in a wealth of shapes and colors*

**Index** . . . . . . . . . . . . . . . . . . . . . . . . . . . . . . 94

# Introduction

Here are the best of all the flowering shrubs and trees profiled by *Fine Gardening* magazine in its first five years of publication.

This clearly illustrated collection includes hundreds of shrubs and trees, ranging from handsome lilacs and viburnums, through hardy magnolias and flowering redbuds, to weeping trees and mighty oaks. The authors recommend tough, rewarding plants that anyone can grow, and stretch your choices with little-known treasures. Among the shrubs and trees discussed here, you are sure to find many that are suited to your property, climate and growing conditions. They'll grace your garden and bring you years of pleasure.

You'll find the articles in this collection especially helpful and inspiring because they are the work of enthusiasts, gardeners who have grown the plants for years and want to help you enjoy them too. Sharing their hard-won experience, the authors tell you the climate and growing conditions each plant needs and explain how to use its shape, size, color and season of bloom to complement the design of your garden.

The editors of *Fine Gardening* hope you'll try the shrubs and trees in this collection of articles. No matter which you choose to grow, your efforts will be rewarded.

"The Best of *Fine Gardening*" series collects articles from back issues of *Fine Gardening* magazine. A note on p. 96 gives the date of first publication for each article; product availability, suppliers' addresses and prices may have changed since then. This book is the second in the series. The first title is *Perennials.*

# Lilacs

## Fragrant blooms from long-lived shrubs

The dense flower clusters of 'Spring Parade', a recent lilac introduction, appear in profusion on a compact shrub.

Daniel K. Ryniec

**L**ilacs are beloved plants. They came from Europe with the earliest settlers and went west with the pioneers as cherished reminders of homes left behind. As the dooryard favorite of our gardening forebears, the common lilac (*Syringa vulgaris*) thrived almost everywhere. A vigorous, woody shrub, it graced the landscape with billowing clusters of flowers and perfumed the spring air with its sweet fragrance.

Modern lilacs offer a wealth of choices for the garden. You can choose from among many species, hybrids and cultivars, ranging in size from dwarfs like the 5-ft. tall 'Miss Kim' to small trees. If you grow early and late-flowering cultivars, the bloom period can start in early spring and end roughly two months later. There are eight distinct colors now: white, violet, blue, lilac, pink, magenta, purple and yellow (if you count the yellow-budded cultivar 'Primrose'). There are also bicolored lilacs such as 'Sensation', which has purple petals dramatically edged in white.

Lilacs are versatile garden plants. When they're covered with flowers, they look great grown as single specimens or surrounded by spring-blooming trees such as dogwoods. They are especially dramatic grouped together in a mass of one color or in contrasting colors. I like combinations of red and white, blue and pink, and purple and white, and I also like to place lilacs with colored flowers against a background of lilacs with white flowers.

I come by my enthusiasm for lilacs firsthand. My parents grew lilacs when we moved westward, like latter-day pioneers, from Massachusetts to Buffalo, New York, and I can remember the fragrance of lilacs from my childhood. Today, I take care of the Louisa Clark Spencer Lilac Collection at the Brooklyn Botanic Garden in New York City. The collection includes 21 species and 130 cultivars. I want to share the experience I've gained so that at least one of the 23 known species and 1,800 varieties of lilacs will find a home in your garden.

**Defining lilacs**

Lilacs are members of the olive family, along with forsythia, privet, jasmine and olives. Two lilacs are European—

'Primrose', the only yellow lilac, actually has creamy-white, single blossoms with pale yellow buds.

## Lilacs (*Syringa*)
si-RING-ga

- Deciduous, flowering shrubs grown as specimens or hedges.
- Showy, often fragrant flowers in clusters from early to late spring.
- Most hardy to USDA Zone 4; grow well to Zone 8 with proper culture.
- Many species and cultivars ranging in size from dwarfs suitable for container growing to medium-sized trees.
- Need full sun and well-drained, fertile loam; established plants are drought-tolerant.

the common lilac, which is a native of Bulgaria and Greece, and the Hungarian lilac (*S. josikaea*). The remaining 20 or so species come from Asia, mainly China.

The common lilac has been extensively hybridized. New cultivars were first introduced in the last century by nurseries like Lemoine of Nancy, France, which developed the so-called French lilacs, whose fragrant, double flowers are among my favorites. Isabella Preston introduced many late-blooming varieties in the early twentieth century. Large shrubs, they grow to 12 ft. tall and have spice-scented pink or lavender flowers. Cultivars include 'W.T. Macoun' and 'Isabella'. Father John L. Fiala, a founding director of the International Lilac Society, bred lilacs for decades until his death in 1990. He introduced 78 cultivars and is responsible for many flower colors other than lilac—deep blues, such as 'Wedgwood Blue' and 'Blue Delft', were his favorites. He

Photo: Susan Kahn; illustration: Rosalind Loeb Wanke

'Paul Hariot', one of the best double, purple lilacs, was hybridized by the French breeder Victor Lemoine and introduced in 1902.

## Tough and rewarding lilacs

| Cultivar or species | Color | Comments |
| --- | --- | --- |
| **Congo** (S. vulgaris) | magenta | single |
| **Donald Wyman** (S. × prestoniae) | purple | single |
| **Excel** (S. × hyacinthiflora) | lilac | single, extremely fragrant |
| **Ivory Silk** (S. reticulata) | white | single, tree lilac, late blooming |
| **Katherine Havemeyer** (S. vulgaris) | pink | double, extremely fragrant |
| **Miss Kim** (S. patula) | purple | single, dwarf plant |
| **President Lincoln** (S. vulgaris) | blue | single, extremely fragrant |
| **Primrose** (S. vulgaris) | yellow | single |
| **Sensation** (S. vulgaris) | purple | single, bicolor |
| **Vestale** (S. vulgaris) | white | single |
| S. reflexa | pink | single |
| S. × persica | lilac | single |

## RESOURCES

*For more information on lilacs, join* **The International Lilac Society** *by writing to secretary Walter W. Oakes, Box 315, Rumford, ME 04276. Annual dues are $15 and membership brings a quarterly journal.*

*A comprehensive reference to lilacs is the book* **Lilacs—The Genus Syringa**, *Fr. John L. Fiala, Timber Press, 9999 SW Wilshire, Portland, OR 97225, 503-292-0745. $63.50 ppd.*

*The following mail-order nurseries sell lilacs for all parts of the country.*

**Ameri-Hort Research,** P.O. Box 1529, Medina, OH 44258. 216-723-4966. (Primarily Fr. Fiala lilacs). Catalog $2, refundable with purchase.

**Buckley Nursery and Garden Center,** 646 N. River Ave., Buckley, WA 98321. 206-829-1811. Catalog free.

**Hastings,** P.O. Box 115535, Atlanta, GA 30310-8535, 404-755-6580. Catalog free.

**Heard Gardens, Ltd.,** 5355 Merle Hay Rd., Johnston, IA 50131, 515-276-4533. Catalog free.

**Wedge Nursery,** Box 114, Rte. 2, Albert Lea, MN 56007, 507-373-5225. Price list free.

also developed early blooming hybrids such as 'Alice Chippo', which has double, lilac-colored blossoms, and late-blooming varieties such as the single, magenta-colored 'Dancing Druid'.

### Lilac culture

If you want to grow lilacs at their best, give them proper culture. They need garden soil with excellent drainage, nearly neutral pH and plenty of organic matter. If you find earthworms when you dig, the soil is probably fine. If necessary, increase the organic matter in your soil by adding composted manure. If drainage is suspect, plant lilacs in a raised bed, or on a hillside. To grow and flower vigorously, lilacs also need unobstructed sunlight for at least six hours a day.

If you buy a bare-root plant, dig a planting hole that's wide enough so you can spread the roots out fully. I add 10-6-4 fertilizer to the backfill at a rate of half a handful for a plant that would fit a 1-qt. pot, and one or two handfuls for a gallon-sized plant.

When you plant container or balled-and-burlapped lilacs, make the planting hole deep enough so the top of the ball or container soil is level with the surrounding soil. Add 10-6-4 fertilizer to the backfill, as for bare-root plants, then fill the hole and water. Spread 2 in. of mulch on the soil, from the drip line to within a few inches of the trunk, to conserve soil moisture and smother weeds.

Water young plants until they're established—roughly three years. Older plants are drought tolerant.

### Maintaining lilacs

Lilacs are easily maintained once they're established. Apply dormant oil in April, before leaves appear, to prevent infestations of scale—tiny, sap-sucking insects. Space plants far enough apart for good air circulation to reduce powdery mildew, which coats lilac leaves with an unsightly, pale film and weakens the plants. Every other year, apply a 10-6-4 fertilizer according to directions and horticultural limestone as needed to maintain a nearly neutral soil pH.

I believe deadheading—removing spent flowers—discourages fungi and viruses because dead flowers, especially on large-flowered lilacs, reduce air circulation through the plant. Be careful not to remove next year's flower buds, which are on the same branch below the dead flower head.

Prune any dead or diseased

Photo: Susan Kahn

branches to encourage healthy growth and flowering. Sterilize pruners between cuts with a 10% solution of bleach and water to prevent the spread of disease. You can prune lilacs after they flower in early June, or in July after the lilac borer (*Podosesia syringae*) lays its eggs. Borers, the larvae of moths, can be found by looking for small holes and sawdust at the base of lilac trunks. They first attack the trunk at the site of injuries, such as those made by mowers and string trimmers. Remove trunks that show signs of borers.

You can rejuvenate old and overgrown lilacs with drastic pruning. In winter, apply 10-6-4 fertilizer and cut large branches to 1 ft. above the ground. Allow only a dozen or so new branches to grow—most growth will come from the base of the old branches. Such drastic pruning may reduce flowering for the next two or three years.

Lilacs that refuse to flower usually have a cultural problem. If you suspect poor drainage, transplant the lilac to a raised bed or other well-drained location. If the plant's in shade, move it to a sunny location or remove the object that is blocking the sunlight. If location, drainage and soil are good and the lilac still isn't blooming, try rejuvenative pruning. As a last resort, replace the plant with a disease- and pollution-resistant variety of *S. × hyacinthiflora* such as 'Anabel' or 'Maiden's Blush'. You could also substitute 'Firmament' or 'Congo', both excellent, older varieties of the common French lilac that tolerate diseases and pollution.

## Choosing lilacs

Although lilac cultivars are sometimes grafted onto privet, ash and common lilac understock, I recommend plants that are on their own roots. If a grafted plant dies to the rootstock, as sometimes happens from disease or cold, you are left with a different plant.

While you should follow your own taste when choosing lilacs, I suggest a few tough, rewarding species and cultivars on p. 10. If you love lilacs as I do, sometimes the name of the variety, like 'Chris', which reminds me of my grandson, is all you need. □

*Daniel K. Ryniec is the former president of the International Lilac Society and tends the lilacs at the Brooklyn Botanic Garden, Brooklyn, New York.*

Photos: above, Skip Kremer; below, Mark Kane

The uniquely marked, bicolor blossoms of the lilac 'Sensation' have reddish-purple florets edged in white. The heady fragrance, heart-shaped leaves and heavy flower clusters of lilacs are among the most welcome garden offerings of spring.

# Tree Peonies

## Breathtaking blossoms on long-lived shrubs

Tree-peony flowers, like those of 'Hinode Sekai' shown above, are a spectacular sight in mid-spring. The flowers are fleeting, but the shrubs are long-lived.

The crepe-paperlike, ruffled petals of 'Hana Kisoi', shown here, are just one striking example of the variation in tree-peony flowers.

## by Anthony De Blasi

met my first tree peony in one of my boyhood haunts, the Brooklyn Botanic Garden in New York. As I wandered into the Japanese Garden area that May, my eyes caught a large shimmery white blossom floating in the air. Upon close inspection, I noticed that the blossom was actually held atop a tall woody stem. Dry botanical descriptions I had read of tree peonies had not prepared me for the stunning sight of a real specimen. It was unlike any herbaceous peony I had seen. The luminous petals, resembling translucent silk, struck a perfect balance between sparseness and opulence. The narrow, deeply divided, gray-green leaves looked artful enough to have been fashioned by a human hand. It's easy to understand why the

Chinese and Japanese have a centuries-old tradition of capturing these precious flowers in embroidery, painting and verse.

Forty years later, I'm still enchanted by tree peonies. I've grown more than 45 kinds of tree peonies in New York, New Hampshire and now Maine. For the beauty of their flowers alone, they head my list of plants to grow in a temperate climate. Even their sculptured leaves are notably attractive—red or purplish when they first unfurl in early spring, gray- or blue-green through most of the growing season, and under favorable conditions red in the autumn. To these virtues, add cold hardiness (roots can survive to -20° to -30°F), simple cultural requirements, longevity and reliable performance. Tree peonies can be grown throughout much of the United States, in USDA Zones 3 through 8. Warmer climates don't provide enough cold for winter dormancy.

### What is a tree peony?

Tree peonies are not trees at all, but are deciduous shrubby perennials. Typically they develop several woody stems, which

Pollen-laden yellow anthers cradled within the yellow and apricot petals of 'Marchioness' add to its beauty. The deeper blush shade at the base of the petals is characteristic of many tree peonies.

may live and increase in size for years or which may be replaced by new stems arising from the roots. In colder climates (north of USDA Zone 6), unprotected stems may die back to the snow line in winter, but even if completely winter-killed they're replaced by new stems in the spring. (Unlike herbaceous-peony stems, tree-peony stems become woody after just one summer of growth.) South of Zone 6, tree-peony stems often persist for many years, but eventually they die off and are replaced. You can expect most tree peonies to grow about 3 ft. to 4 ft. tall and spread at least equally as wide. Unchecked by cold, they can reach more than 6 ft. tall, and spread a bit wider.

Extensive hybridization and cultivar selection has resulted in an astonishing array of flower color, from blackish-red through shades of pink to yellow and even cream. In the center of the petals sits a prominently displayed golden crown of anthers. The flowers are quite large, typically 8 in. to 10 in. in diameter. They vary remarkably in texture and appearance: smooth or crinkled; velvety, silky or satiny; wavy, twisted or frilled; wispy or sturdy;

single, semidouble or double. The reddish-purple flowers and some of the pinks have a lovely rose perfume, and several of the yellow-flowered hybrids exude a citrus fragrance. Other tree-peony flowers emit a pungent, piney odor.

Usually one flower is formed per stem, generally near the top. Each flower remains open for five to seven days, but since the flowers open at different times, the bloom period of an individual plant can last up to ten days. You can extend the season to about one month by planting cultivars and hybrids with overlapping bloom periods. Some of my favorite tree peonies are listed in the box on p. 14.

Tree peonies are native to China, and both the Chinese and Japanese have developed many hybrids and cultivars. The most commonly available and probably the most popular tree peonies are Japanese cultivars of *Paeonia suffruticosa*. These have the finest foliage and bearing—their stems stand upright in a stately fashion. Their flowers, available in white, purple, or shades of pink and red, sometimes have a deeper tint radiating around the anthers. The Japanese cultivars are the earliest tree peonies to bloom. In my garden in Long Island, New York (USDA Zone 7), they normally opened about the third week of May. Here in West Newfield, Maine (borderline of Zones 4 and 5), they flower the first or second week of June. (All tree peonies bloom about ten weeks after they leaf out.) The Chinese cultivars of *P. suffruticosa* are worth searching for, though they're not easy to find. Their blossoms are so full that they bend under their own weight.

*P. lutea* hybrids, bred mostly in Europe and America, are best known for their yellow flowers, sometimes with red or pink shades, but this group also includes red, lavender and pink flowers suffused with yellow, black-red, coppery hues and sunset tints, and often dark-red flares at the base of the petals. (*The American Tree Peony*, a book available for $25 postpaid from the American Peony Society, contains good color photos of these hybrids. See Resources, facing page, for the society's address.)

Generally the flowers of *P. lutea* hybrids have a nodding rather than upright habit. The heavy double flowers of some can droop so much that they're hidden in the foliage, which is usually bushier than that of the Japanese cultivars of *P. suffruticosa*. Though they aren't invasive, *P. lutea* hybrids tend to spread more underground than Japanese cultivars, which have a fleshy root.

### Buying and growing tree peonies

Tree peonies used to be relatively obscure, enormously expensive plants that connoisseurs hunted down. Today many fine tree peonies can be purchased by mail order or at local nurseries. Unfortunately, a good many of the most desirable cultivars aren't available in the trade, but I hope more nurseries will become interested in reviving these masterpieces.

Tree peonies are propagated by bud-grafting the desired cultivar onto the rootstock of an herbaceous peony. At least two years is needed to produce a saleable plant. Depending on the age of the plant and whether the nursery propagates in-house or imports, plants can cost as little as $12 or as much as $60. Even at the high end, I think that's a reasonable price to pay for a spectacular plant that will probably outlive me.

Tree peonies typically bloom two to three years after transplanting, though they may bloom sparsely as soon as the first spring after planting. Don't be tempted to buy an older specimen that's already reached flowering age—it's much less likely to survive transplanting.

**Selecting a site**—Tree peonies are rugged and adaptable, but they fare best in uncrowded quarters, free from root competition. Since they can spread up to 6 ft., plant them at least 12 ft. from the nearest tree and at least 2 ft. to 3 ft. from a wall. Too much sun burns the petals and too much wind batters and breaks the stems, so the plants must be protected from both. Choose a location that's shaded from midday and afternoon sun, or be prepared to temporarily shade the plants during the blooming season. A well-placed beach umbrella or lath enclosure does the trick. A wall provides much better wind protection than a hedge, whose roots might interfere with those of the tree peony. If you plant your tree peonies out in the open, tether the main stems to a nonrusting metal stake as they develop.

Beyond these considerations, placing tree peonies in the landscape depends on aesthetics. I'm a collector, not a landscaper. To me, tree peonies are not plants to use, but ones to appreciate. So I like to place them where I can approach them from all angles and view them clearly up close or from afar. I've grown tree peonies at the edge of an oak grove, shaded from the midday sun; along a low stone wall; and close to the house, where their tops are protected from wind and severe cold.

You can use tree peonies in your landscape much like any other shrub, as long as they're given top billing with no competition, visual or otherwise. They look lovely planted in

'Renkaku' (white) and 'Suigan' (pink) are two handsome tree peonies recommended for the landscaper.

## Recommended tree peonies

The following are some of my favorite tree peonies. All are available from one or more of the mail-order sources given on the facing page. Each listing includes the cultivar or hybrid name; an English translation of any Japanese name; "S" indicating *P. suffruticosa* cultivars or "L" indicating *P. lutea* hybrids; and distinctive characteristics.

**'Age of Gold'**—L; semidouble flower; butter-yellow rosettes with ruffled petals; vigorous, bushy plant.

**'Gaugin'**—L; single; yellow heavily suffused with red veins.

**'Hana Kisoi' ('Floral Rivalry')**—S; semidouble; pink shading deeper toward center, frilly petals; tall plant.

**'Hinode Sekai' ('World of the Rising Sun')**—S; semidouble; rose-red with crinkled petals; fragrant; heavy bloom from dwarf plant.

**'Kamada Nishiki' ('Kamada Brocade')**—S; semidouble; rich purple with buds like tea roses.

**'Marchioness'**—L; semidouble; blend of yellow, apricot and rose with dark flares; wavy petals of heavy substance; floriferous.

**'Renkaku' ('Flight of Cranes')**—S; semidouble; elegant white chalices; tall plant.

**'Rimpo' ('Sacred Bird')**—S; double; dark purple with velvety nap and fluted petals; tall plant.

**'Rock's Variety'**—S; semidouble; white with dark purple at petal base, fluffy; vigorous plant.

**'Shintenchi' ('New Heaven and Earth')**—S; semidouble; orchid pink with deeper shades toward center, edges fading to silver, rose-red flares at petal base.

**'Silver Sails'**—L; single; pale silvery-yellow, faintly flushed red with similarly colored flares.

**'Yachiyo Tsubaki' ('Long Hedge of Camellias')**—S; semidouble; coral, silky; tall, slender plant.          —A.DB.

Photo: Anthony De Blasi

'Gaugin' (above) and 'Shintenchi' (below) illustrate the dramatic range of tree-peony flower colors.

## RESOURCES

For more information about tree peonies, join the **American Peony Society**, 250 Interlachen Rd., Hopkins, MN 55343. The annual membership fee ($7.50, individual; $10.00, family) includes four bulletins per year.

Tree-peony availability varies depending on time of year. Some mail-order sources are:

**Caprice Farm Nursery**, 15425 S.W. Pleasant Hill Rd., Sherwood, OR 97140. 503-625-7241. Catalog $1.00.

**Kelly Nurseries**, Catalog Division, Louisiana, MO 63353. 314-754-4525. Catalog free.

**Klehm Nursery**, Rt. 5, Box 197, South Barrington, IL 60010. 312-551-3720. Catalog $4.00.

**Reath's Nursery**, 100 Central Blvd., Vulcan, MI 49892. 800-553-3715. Catalog $1.00.

**Wayside Gardens**, Garden Lane, Hodges, SC 29695. 800-845-1124. Catalog free.

**White Flower Farm**, Litchfield, CT 06759. 800-888-7756. Catalog $5.00.

**Van Bourgondien Brothers**, 245 Farmingdale Rd., P.O. Box A, Babylon, NY 11702. 800-873-9444. Catalog free.

borders, along steps, next to a gate or near a statue. Don't mass them in beds; their uniqueness will be lost.

A word of caution: The stems persist through the winter, looking quite shabby, much like a bunch of twigs stuck in the ground. You can mitigate this effect somewhat by camouflaging the plants with pine boughs, or by letting them go to seed and enjoying the pods.

**Planting**—Tree peonies must have a well-drained, moisture-retentive soil, preferably neutral to slightly acid. Avoid areas where water stands, even if just for a brief period. Soil lacking in these qualities may be replaced with a homemade mix of about equal parts topsoil, compost and peat moss. Plant tree peonies in September or October, to give their roots time to get established before the ground freezes. Avoid spring planting unless the tree peonies are growing in containers when you buy them.

For each plant, I dig a hole 2 ft. wide and equally deep, setting aside any sod and good soil and hauling away the rest. Then I toss the sod and good soil into the bottom of the hole, and fill nearly to the top with my homemade mix, stirring in 2 lb. of bone meal per plant.

There are two tricks to planting. First, set the junction between stem(s) and roots 5 in. below grade. This encourages the cultivar to form its own roots above those of the herbaceous-peony understock, minimizing the chance of the understock taking over. When the hole is filled the proper amount, position the plant and fill in around it. Second, do not pound down the soil around the plant, as is frequently recommended. Instead, leave the soil loose and flood the hole with water. (This is easier to do if the hole is not quite filled with soil.) After the water has drained, add enough soil mix to fill the hole completely, make a slight mound of loose soil around the plant and mulch with a coarse layer of leaves or other material. A low barrier of boards or hardware cloth set around each plant until the ground freezes will keep away unauthorized diggers who are attracted to the soft soil. Repeated transplanting eventually takes its toll on tree peonies. And unlike most perennials, they're not revitalized by division.

**Care**—You don't grow tree peonies—you let them grow. Peonies resent pushing; don't force-feed them. An annual dressing of bone meal, sprinkled lightly and scratched into the soil around each plant right after bloom, is sufficient fertilizer. I once went on a superphosphate kick—I got more blooms, but they were small and inferior-looking. Likewise, high-nitrogen fertilizers and foliar feeding are out, as they push vegetative growth.

Rainfall has always provided enough moisture wherever I've grown tree peonies. Even in droughty weather, it's still best to let nature take its course unless you're prepared to take charge and water the plants deeply and regularly. You'll definitely need to water if you live in a hot climate. You'll also probably have to shade the plants more, especially in midday.

To help retain moisture and suppress weeds, I keep a 2-in. layer of mulch, such as dried grass clippings, around the plants. I never let nearby lawn encroach either. I hand-hoe—I don't use herbicides—but in spring I'm careful not to chop off any new stems emerging from the ground.

Tree peonies need no pruning other than the removal of dead wood. You may cut off the seed heads, down to the nearest bud, but doing so is purely cosmetic. If the understock sends up

a shoot, or sucker, which it rarely does, dig into the soil and cut away the sucker and the section of root attached to it. The suckers will have broader foliage than the rest of the plant, resembling that of herbaceous peonies.

If you live in a sub-zero winter climate, as I do, protect your plants from the cold by surrounding them with wooden or wire frames filled with oak leaves, pine twigs or other coarse mulch. Snow is an excellent insulator, but it may be either too shallow to cover the tops of the plants or so deep that it crushes them. Remember to firmly stake the main woody (not green) stems well before the onset of winter.

While a tree peony adjusts to its new home and gathers energy, it may not do what you expect it to do. The flower buds may not swell and open, and if they do, the flowers may be off-color or just not live up to their reputation. A stem may suddenly wilt and die. (If so, simply remove it.) As with shrubs like lilacs and rhododendrons, tree peonies take a few years to get going. It's worth the wait.

Precise regimens, useful as they are, keep us from treating the cultivation of ornamentals as an art. There's always room for experiment and discovery. For years I recommended never planting a tree peony near the foundation of a house. I should have said hardly ever, since now I have a thriving specimen just 2 ft. from my house, despite the potential problems of heat buildup, rapidly drying soil, confinement and leaching of unwanted minerals from the foundation. To me, how plants respond or don't respond to the rules is part of the fun of gardening.

To protect his tree peonies from strong winds and winter cold, author De Blasi planted several snugged up close to his house. 'High Noon' drapes over the lawn, while just one plant of 'Age of Gold' has filled in near the stairs.

## Pests and diseases

Tree peonies are remarkably unsusceptible to disease and insect damage, but you should be on the lookout for a few problems. In very wet spring weather, a fungal disease, botrytis, may wilt young shoots and turn them black. Where such conditions prevail, spray with a recommended fungicide, such as benomyl, once when the young shoots emerge and then two and four weeks later.

When leaves are still tender, I watch for a variety of nibblers, most of them larval forms of insects, and I handpick them. My worst insect pest is the arboreal cutworm, which loves to dine on developing flower buds. We meet at night, under the beam of a flashlight, for a lesson in table manners. In some areas, carpenter bees (which resemble bumblebees, but have bald instead of furry abdomens) bore into cut stem ends to build their egg cells. You can easily exclude them by plugging all cuts with chewing gum or grafting wax.

I don't spray to control insects. I've found that their attacks are few and far between in a healthy garden, where a diversity of species planted in their preferred locations are accompanied by a team of birds and beneficial insects. Some call this organic gardening; I call it practical.

On warm, sunny days, I am moved to shade the flowers of my exposed tree peonies with beach umbrellas, to prolong their magic. On rainy days, I have an excuse to pick the flowers and flaunt them throughout the house, floating in bowls. Is it worth the bother? Like the infrequent, crystal-clear view of a noble mountain normally shrouded in mist, yes!  □

*Anthony De Blasi grows tree peonies in West Newfield, Maine.*

Photo: Anthony De Blasi

# Viburnums
## Handsome foliage, white flowers and bright berries grace a durable shrub

by Rick Bogusch

Viburnums are among the most beautiful, versatile and undemanding shrubs I know. In late spring or early summer, they are bedecked with large, showy clusters of white, cream or pink-tinged flowers delicately accented by golden stamens. The flowers cover the shrubs from top to bottom for two to three weeks, and some cultivars offer a spicy, carnation-like fragrance. By late summer or fall, shiny red, yellow, blue or black berries festoon the plants, and remain colorful through winter. Usually, however, the berries are devoured by birds and other wildlife, who seem to find them especially delectable.

Few shrubs can match viburnum's handsome, healthy leaves, which earn the plants a place in the landscape even when they're not in fruit or flower. Viburnum leaves range from shiny to felty, leathery to deeply-veined, and from the darkest green through rich medium green to gray in color. As a bonus, the foliage of most deciduous viburnums turns brilliant yellow-orange to red-purple in the fall. And their gray-brown, twiggy framework, often covered with a soft felt, makes viburnums attractive even after they've lost their leaves.

Viburnums are widely adapted and versatile. There are deciduous viburnums hardy enough to survive frigid northern winters and evergreen viburnums that thrive in the hot and humid South. Many viburnums become medium-size shrubs, about 6 ft. to 8 ft. tall and equally wide, but others grow much larger or smaller. A few

Jeweled with red berries atop lustrous leaves, Wright viburnum is a brilliant addition to the landscape. Few shrubs are as adaptable or easy to grow as viburnums.

The creamy white flowers of 'Erie' highlight its dark green leaves, offering a bright spot for a shady corner of a garden.

viburnums even have the habit of a small tree. Here at Cornell Plantations, the arboretum of Cornell University in Ithaca, New York, where I work as a landscape designer, I've used viburnums with equal success as single specimens, in perennial borders, combined with other flowering shrubs, as screens, as hedges and in naturalized areas.

I'd like to encourage you to try viburnums— I think you'll find them as rewarding as I do. They're commonly available at nurseries and garden centers. Several large, wholesale nurseries carry a wide selection, so if you can't find the one you're looking for, ask your local nursery to special order it for you.

## Viburnums
### (Viburnum spp.)
vye-BURR-num

- Small-to-large deciduous, semi-evergreen or evergreen shrubs.

- Hardy to Zone 2 or 3, depending on species or cultivar. Most can be grown through Zone 7 or 8, a few in Zone 10.

- White or pink-tinged springtime flowers, sometimes fragrant

- Red, yellow, blue or black berries, and yellow-orange to red-purple fall foliage.

- Thrive in full sun or bright, open shade. Tolerate wide range of soils.

A close look at a flower cluster of 'Mohawk' reveals its deep red buds, which open to petals that are white on the inside and red on the outside. The spicy aroma perfumes the landscape all day.

## Choosing a viburnum

Before you choose a viburnum for your garden, consider your climate and growing conditions. You should also visit local nurseries, arboreta or botanic gardens to learn more about the best viburnums for your area. I have room here to list only a sampling of viburnum species and cultivars. (See the chart on p. 21. For a longer list—26 viburnum species and cultivars—please send a long,

stamped, self-addressed envelope to Kerry O'Neil, *Fine Gardening*, P.O. Box 5506, Newtown, CT 06470-5506.)

The deciduous viburnums are the hardiest, some of them tolerating the winter lows of USDA Hardiness Zone 2 (-50°F). The evergreens and semi-evergreens are hardy only to Zone 5 (-20°F). Here at Cornell Plantations, in Zone 5, with some sections of the arboretum equivalent to a zone colder or warmer, we can grow most of the deciduous viburnums, some of the hardiest semi-evergreen species and one or two of the evergreen ones.

Most viburnums prefer full sun and will bloom most abundantly if they have it. Many will also grow into lush,

Photos: Larry Albee; illustration: Rosalind Loeb Wanke

**The white flowers of 'Shasta' seem to float on its graceful, tiered branches. Like most viburnums, 'Shasta' grows well in open shade or sun.**

floriferous shrubs in bright shade like that under high-canopied trees. However, nearly all viburnums tolerate part shade, and some may require it if your summers are especially torrid. Arrowwood viburnum *(Viburnum dentatum)* seems to be the most shade-tolerant.

Choose species or cultivars that can reach their mature size without being crowded by nearby plants or buildings. Most viburnums look best if they're allowed to achieve their natural forms without pruning.

## Small viburnums

There aren't many viburnums that grow under 5 ft. tall, but those that do are perfect for foundation plantings or other restricted spaces. The compact Koreanspice viburnum *(V. carlesii* 'Compactum'), a rounded shrub which grows about 2½ ft. to 3½ ft. tall and equally wide, is about the only small viburnum for those of us in harsh-winter climates, and it's a prize. In late April or early May, its pink buds open into dome-shaped (semi-snowball), fragrant, white flower clusters. It's ideal along-side a walkway, where you can appreciate its spicy scent. This deciduous cultivar, which can be grown from

Zones 4 (-30°F) through 7 or 8, bears dark green leaves that turn purple-red in fall. The fruits are insignificant, as on other semi-snowball types. Look for the Hoogendorn strain. It's the most vigorous and nicely-shaped. However, like all compact Koreanspice viburnums, it is grafted onto an understock that can easily overgrow it, so cut off all sprouts arising from beneath the graft.

## Medium viburnums

Burkwood viburnum *(V. × burkwoodii)*, bears semi-snowball, white, fragrant flowers and lustrous, dark green foliage that turns wine-red in cold climates. This species thrives from Zone 4 through 8. From Zone 6 south, it retains much of its foliage throughout winter, but in colder areas, the plants are deciduous, except in the most protected locations. Grouping several plants of this species together for cross-pollination encourages more fruiting, though the crops are never outstanding.

Burkwood viburnum is very tolerant of air pollution, making it an excellent shrub for urban areas. A good companion for broad-leaved evergreens or other shrubs, this species grows 8 ft. to 10 ft. tall and 6 ft. to 8 ft. wide, though many of its cultivars are more compact. They all tend to become a bit straggly with age and need occasional pruning to maintain a neat appearance.

If you're looking for an abundant display of colorful fruit, there are no better deciduous shrubs than linden viburnum (*V. dilatatum*) and its cultivars. The smallest and perhaps the most dependable is 'Erie', which grows into a neatly rounded shrub about 6 ft. to 8 ft. tall and 6 ft. to 10 ft. wide. Its bright red fruits are so numerous that they bend its branches to the ground. In late May or early June, creamy white flower clusters cover its dark green, hairy leaves, which turn orange-red and yellow in fall. Well suited to Zones 4 or 5 through 7, 'Erie' is appealing as a specimen or in a shrub border.

If you're looking for a tough, indestructible, medium-sized shrub that will grow just about anywhere, arrowwood viburnum is for you. This North American native, which is hardy to Zone 2 and can be grown as far south as Zone 8, forms dense stands as it colonizes old, abandoned fields. In the landscape, it is especially useful for naturalizing, for informal hedges and screens and for planting in masses. It domesticates well, usually growing 6 ft. to 8 ft. tall and 6 ft. to 10 ft. wide in cultivation. To renew this species, you can cut it back to the ground and it will grow back more vigorously than before. Arrowwood is not as showy as other viburnums, but it's still garden-worthy, with creamy white flower clusters in May and June, attractive blue fruits in September, and shiny, dark green leaves that turn yellow to dark red to red-purple in fall.

## Large viburnums

'Willowwood' and 'Allegheny', cultivars of lantanaphyllum viburnum (*V. × rhytidophylloides*), merit a place in the landscape planted in masses or as specimens, screens, informal hedges, or as foundation plants. Their leaves are their most attractive feature—dark green and leathery above and felted with dense, light gray-brown hairs below. Though deciduous, 'Willowwood' and 'Allegheny' may hold their leaves into November, even in very cold weather, and in mild years can carry their leaves into spring. Both do well in Zones 4 through 8, producing an abundance of creamy white flower clusters in May followed in September by red fruits that gradually darken to black.

'Willowwood' is the more vigorous of the two, growing up to 15 ft. tall and 15 ft. wide. It becomes attractively leggy with age and can easily accommodate ferns, hostas and other shade-loving ground covers under its arching branches. 'Allegheny', a more globose plant, can reach 11 ft. tall and 12 ft. wide.

Doublefile viburnum (*V. plicatum* f. *tomentosum*) is considered one of the most beautiful flowering shrubs in existence, and it's not hard to see why. Layer upon layer of horizontally tiered branches are lushly clothed with large, dark green leaves that hang straight down and turn deep red-purple in fall. Glistening white, flat-topped

Southern blackhaw, one of the few tree-like viburnums, displays shiny fall foliage.

If birds don't devour them first, the yellow fruits of *Viburnum opulus* 'Xanthocarpum' (facing page) will soon look even more striking after the leaves have fully turned purple and red.

flower clusters, 4 in. to 6 in. wide, appear in late May or early June. (The clusters, which resemble lace caps, are composed of small, fruit-producing flowers surrounded by larger, showy, sterile flowers that attract insect pollinators.) Fruits turn red in July, then gradually darken to black if the birds don't eat them first.

'Shasta', a compact, doublefile viburnum that grows 6 ft. tall and 12 ft. wide, is dependably hardy to Zone 4, while the species is hardy just to Zone 5. Like all double-files, 'Shasta' makes a great corner foundation planting.

## Planting and care

Ample moisture is perhaps the only requirement for growing healthy viburnums. Most viburnums prefer soil that is well drained, but not too dry. They need about 1 in. of water per week during the growing season. During dry spells, it's wise to water them deeply once a week. They grow best in deep, loamy soils enriched with organic matter, but they'll also grow well in soils of average fertility. Our soils are mostly heavy clays or gravelly loams, and the viburnums do just fine.

Give new plants a generous hole and a fertile growing medium. We usually plant in a large hole that is 3 ft. to 4 ft. wide and about 2½ ft. deep, and we backfill it with stone-free soil enriched with rotted manure or compost, peat moss and a fertilizer formulated for shrubs. We mulch with shredded bark, keep the plants well watered during the first growing season, and replace the mulch and fertilize every other year.

Viburnums are generally vigorous, trouble-free shrubs, living about ten to 20 years in the average landscape planting. Some, like Siebold viburnum (*V. sieboldii*), last much longer. By and large, viburnums have few pest problems, especially if they aren't subjected to excessive temperature or drought stress. Leaf spot, a bacterial disease, can become a problem with the Koreanspice viburnums. The cranberry bush types, so called because of the color and the appearance of their fruit, are prone to aphid infestations, especially the European species (*V. opulus*).

As a rule, viburnums should not be heavily pruned, but you may need to occasionally remove crossing branches or wayward twigs. To renew growth on old viburnums, you can selectively remove some of the large, older branches at the base, which will encourage the growth of vigorous new shoots. Viburnums bloom on new wood, so prune after they flower.  □

*Rick Bogusch is the landscape designer at Cornell Plantations in Ithaca, New York.*

Photos: above, Harrison Flint; facing page, Susan Kahn

## A Selection of Viburnums

| Botanical name | Common name | USDA Hardiness Zone– southern limit | Mature size (height × width in feet) | Flowers | Fruit | Foliage d = deciduous se = semi-evergreen e = evergreen | Landscape uses |
|---|---|---|---|---|---|---|---|
| **Small** | | | | | | | |
| ***Viburnum davidii*** | David viburnum | 8-10 | 3-5 × 5 | white | bright blue | **e** | foundation, shrub border |
| *V.* 'Eskimo' | Service viburnum | 6-8 | 4-5 × 5 | white | red, black | **se** | foundation, shrub border |
| **Medium** | | | | | | | |
| *V.* × *burkwoodii* 'Mohawk' | Burkwood viburnum | 4-10 | 7-8 × 8-9 | white/red; red buds; fragrant | insignificant | **d/se** | shrub border |
| *V.* × *juddii* | Judd viburnum | 4-8 | 6-8 × 6-8 | white; pink buds; fragrant | insignificant | **d** | foundation, accent |
| *V. trilobum* 'Alfredo' | American cranberry bush viburnum | 2-7 | 5 × 5-6 | white | red, variable fruit set | **d** | foundation, specimen informal hedge |
| *V. wrightii* | Wright viburnum | 5-7 | 6-10 × 8-10 | white | red | **d** | foundation, shrub border, screen |
| **Large** | | | | | | | |
| *V. tinus* | Laurustinus viburnum | 8-10 | 6-12 × 6-10 | white; pink buds | metallic blue | **e** | hedge, screen, masses |
| *V. opulus* 'Notcutt' | European cranberry bush | 3-8 | 8-12 × 10-15 | white | red | **d** | shrub border, screen |
| *V. opulus* 'Xanthocarpum' | Yellow-fruited European cranberry bush | 3-8 | 8-10 × 10-12 | white | yellow | **d** | specimen, shrub border. informal hedge |
| *V.* × *pragense* | Prague viburnum | 5-8 | 10 × 10 or larger | creamy white; slightly fragrant | red to black | **e** | foundation, accent, screen |
| *V. sargentii* 'Onondaga' | Sargent viburnum | 3-7 | 6 × 6 or larger | white with maroon tinge; red buds | bright red | **d** | foundation, specimen, screen, mass |
| *V. sieboldii* | Siebold viburnum | 4-7 | 15-20 × 12-15 | creamy white | red to black | **d** | small tree |
| *V. rufidulum* | Southern or rusty blackhaw | 5-9 | 10-20 × 10-20 or larger | creamy white | blue-black | **e** | naturalizing, shrub border, small tree |

Like the European and Asian horse chestnuts to which they are closely related, native buckeyes put on a stunning annual flower show. The flower panicles of the June-blooming bottlebrush buckeye are particularly dramatic because they are so large, growing to 20 in. long.

Buckeyes seem most content in the high shade of neighboring trees. In the photo on the facing page, the white panicles of bottlebrush buckeyes brighten a lightly shaded corner of a garden.

# Buckeyes

## These easy-care shrubs deserve wider attention

by Larry P. Lowman

Some landscape plants are so finicky that you must find just the right niche for them in your garden. Then you have to pamper them—and still you're not quite sure of success. If you'd prefer less demanding plants, consider one of the native buckeyes. Here in Arkansas they are among the most rugged, adaptable and beautiful woody plants I know.

Buckeyes are distinctive both in leaf and in flower. They have unusual leaves, consisting of five, and occasionally seven, individual leaflets. The leaflets, which vary in size from 3 in. to 6 in. long, radiate from a central petiole, or leaf stem, like fingers from a hand (an arrangement that botanists term "palmately compound"). The small, tubular flowers appear in early spring grouped in showy clusters, or panicles, which stand upright on the branches. On closer inspection, each individual flower in the panicle resembles a miniature orchid with its long tube, flaring mouth and lipped petals. The flowers come in red, white, cream, greenish-yellow and pink.

There are at least five or six species of native buckeyes, all belonging to the genus *Aesculus*. There are also foreign members of the genus, commonly called horse chestnuts. One of these, the European horse chestnut, is a large shade tree that is widely planted in the eastern United States. I won't talk about the horse chestnuts here, nor will I describe the native yellow buckeye (*Aesculus octandra*, also known as *A. flava*), which attains proportions equal to a stately oak. I will focus, instead, on four shrub-

Photos these 2 pages: Michael A. Dirr
Illustration: Rosalind L. Wanke

---

### Buckeye *(Aesculus)*

- Shrub to medium-sized tree growing 10 ft. to 40 ft. tall.
- Hardy in USDA Zones 3 to 7, depending on species; most will perform well in warmer climates.
- Most species leaf out and flower before other woody plants.
- Compound leaves are made up of five to seven leaflets.
- Flowers are tubular in shape and arranged in spire-like panicles; red, white, cream, greenish-yellow or pink in color.
- Grow in light shade or sun in average soil.
- The nuts, or buckeyes, are poisonous.

---

by buckeyes that I believe merit more use in the residential landscape.

**Red buckeye**—Red buckeye (*Aesculus pavia*), a multi-stemmed shrub or small tree rarely exceeding 10 ft. in height or spread, was the first species I encountered in the woods around my childhood home in central Arkansas. Even as a young child I delighted in the unfurling buds and blossoms of this woodland shrub. I still consider red buckeye among the superlative beauties of spring in our local forests.

Red buckeye is precocious, showing its leaves before any other tree does. Beginning in March here in Arkansas (USDA Zone 7), the buds swell to enormous size—larger than jellybeans—and turn rose-pink. As the translucent bud scales expand and spread apart and the reddish-purple new leaves emerge, the bud-tipped twigs look so beautiful that people unfamiliar with buckeyes think they are flowering. Soon enough the real show begins, as clusters of flower buds emerge above the leaves, elongate into 4-in.- to 8-in.-tall panicles and finally open to brilliant red blossoms.

Red buckeye is native throughout the Southeast, from Oklahoma to the Atlantic, north to the Missouri bootheel and into Virginia, but it can be hardy in gardens in Zones 4 or 5, if you collect seeds from plants growing in the northern limits of its range. It's at its best under a woodland canopy in humus-rich soil, but it will thrive almost anywhere. I find few native shrubs are more adaptable. In sun or shade, in conditions moist or dry, in soil rich or poor, the red buckeye performs.

**Ohio buckeye**—In the Ozark Mountains and throughout the Midwest, the Ohio buckeye (*Aesculus glabra*) predominates. Hardy to Zone 3, the Ohio buckeye can also take the summer heat of Zones 7 or 8. It is similar in foliage and habit to the red buckeye, but it has yellow flowers, sometimes accented with bright orange stamens or orange markings on the petals. This species also grows larger than the red buckeye. The Ohio buckeye can become a 20-ft. to 40-ft. tree, but in my experience here in Arkansas, it rarely grows larger than a big shrub or small tree.

Some reference books say that the Ohio buckeye is subject to several diseases and pests. I've never had a problem that required treatment. I suspect that many of the problems associated with this buckeye are, in fact, attributable to the early yellowing of the leaves, which is normal. But before planting this buckeye, you may want to ask a local cooperative extension agent if it is known to suffer from any major problems in your area.

In late summer both red buckeyes and Ohio buckeyes bear a shiny, brown nut that looks like a chestnut. Beware of this resemblance, however, because the fresh nuts, also called buckeyes, are poisonous. Nevertheless, considerable folklore persists about carrying a "lucky buckeye" in your pocket—for good luck or to keep away rheumatism or some other evil. Some Ozarks residents have carried the same buckeye in their pocket or purse every day for years.

Both of these buckeyes must be

placed judiciously in the landscape. They are among the first woody plants to leaf out in spring. Correspondingly, both species also develop yellowish fall color and drop their leaves quite early, as soon as late July or early August in my area. This retreat into early dormancy may surprise the uninitiated,

Humans are not alone in their appreciation of buckeyes. Here a northern oriole stops to sample the nectar of a red buckeye in Columbia, Missouri. If the timing of the flowering is right, red buckeyes will also attract hummingbirds.

The red buckeye is one of the first deciduous shrubs to leaf out and flower in spring. Against the backdrop of its compound leaves, the brilliant red flowers dazzle winter-weary eyes.

who might think that the plants are dying. And the fastidious landscaper might object to the sight of bare branches so many weeks before other deciduous plants drop their leaves. It's true that these buckeyes would not be the plant of choice in a formal foundation planting. However, if massed in an informal garden, used as an accent in a naturalistic landscape design or included as understory plants in woodland sites, these buckeyes will put on a spectacular spring display without detracting from the landscape when bare of leaves. And, as if to make their early dormancy more palatable, both species have attractive, silvery bark and an unusual branching pattern that reminds me of abstract wire sculpture.

Perhaps even the foliage drawback can be overcome. A red buckeye is occasionally found in southern Arkansas and northern Louisiana that does not flower until May or June and has glossy, dark green foliage which remains attractive until fall. Selected plants of this variety (which some botanical references cite as a separate species, *Aesculus splendens*) are now in the hands of nurserymen, and introductions are sure to be forthcoming.

**California buckeye**—The California buckeye (*Aesculus californica*) is native to central California. It is a multi-stemmed shrub, quite similar in size and appearance to the red buckeye. But its striking flowers are white, sometimes tinged with variable amounts of pink, and each individual blossom is somewhat larger than the red buckeye's. In addition, the foliage has a distinctly bluish hue.

Like the red and Ohio buckeyes, the California buckeye leafs out early and, responding to its hot, dry summer environment, usually drops its foliage in midsummer. As a result, it,

## SOURCES

*Few mail-order nurseries carry more than one of the buckeyes discussed by the author. The following growers, with one exception, list at least three species.*

**Eastern Plant Specialities,** Box 226, Georgetown, ME 04548, 207-371-2888. *Aesculus pavia, A. glabra* and *A. parviflora*. Catalog $1, refundable.

**Forestfarm,** 990 Tetherow Rd., Williams, OR 97544. *Aesculus pavia, A. glabra* and *A. californica*. Catalog $3.

**Las Pilitas Nursery,** Star Route Box 23X, Santa Margarita, CA 93453, 805-438-5992. Only source of *Aesculus californica* in California. Price list free.

**Woodlanders, Inc.,** 1128 Colleton Ave., Aiken, SC 29801, 803-648-7522. *Aesculus pavia, A. glabra* and *A. parviflora*. Catalog $1. New catalog in September.

Photos: top: Gay Bumgarner; below: Pamela Harper

too, requires careful placement in the landscape to permit enjoyment of its spring show without drawing too much attention to its early leaf drop.

The ultimate cold hardiness of the California buckeye is still open to question. What is known for certain is that it briefly withstands single-digit temperatures in its native habitat. Whether it will tolerate colder winter temperatures or survive the late spring cold snaps that are common in southern states remains to be seen. I'm encouraged by the performance of several plants that I started from seed here at my nursery in Zone 7. The temperature this past December dipped to -4°F, but the California buckeyes leafed out nicely this spring.

**Bottlebrush buckeye**—The aristocrat of North American buckeyes is the bottlebrush buckeye (*Aesculus parviflora*), a shrubby species native to the Deep South. Not well known among gardeners and landscapers, this overlooked gem has all of the desirable traits of the red, Ohio and California buckeyes and none of their drawbacks.

The bottlebrush buckeye brings pizzazz to the summer garden. It bears spectacular 12-in.- to 20-in.-long, white flower panicles over a three- to four-week period in June and July. The orange-tipped stamens protrude beyond the petals, giving the panicles their unusual brush-like appearance and the plant its name. The foliage is a rich green, and remains so until autumn, when it turns the same lovely gold as the leaves of the ginkgo tree. It is hardy as far north as Zone 4. At the same time, it performs well in much warmer climates, though in Zones 7 through 9 it should be afforded some afternoon shade to prevent leaf scorch during very hot weather.

This buckeye thrives in the dappled shade of hardwoods or sparely-branched conifers. A single, large specimen or grouping in bloom is stunning. Because the bottlebrush buckeye spreads actively by sending out basal sprouts and low branches that root where they touch the ground, allow room for it in your garden. Over the course of 20 years, a healthy specimen may grow to the size and shape of a haystack, 8 ft. to 10 ft. high by 15 ft. to 20 ft. across.

### Starting buckeyes from seed
You can purchase buckeye plants from mail-order nurseries (see Sources on opposite page), but they are also easy to start from seeds. You can collect seeds from wild populations, if you live in the native range of the buckeye you want to grow, or from a friend's plants.

The nuts of red, Ohio and bottlebrush buckeyes are viable (alive and capable of sprouting) for only a few hours to a week or so after they have fallen from the tree. So it's important to gather them as soon as the pouch surrounding the nut begins to split, usually in late summer. Sow the buckeyes immediately in groups of two or three at a depth of 1 in. to 2 in. where you want the plant to grow. The seeds sprout immediately and send their radical (taproot) several inches into the soil. Only a small bud appears above

The opening of the Ohio buckeye's buds in early spring is a wondrous event. The leaves and the flower buds pop up and out in a slow-motion explosion. Over the next few weeks the leaves will grow to their mature size, while the flower panicle swells, reaches upward and finally opens its yellow, tube-shaped flowers.

ground. Top growth starts from this bud the following spring.

The seeds of the California buckeye are viable for a longer time than those of other buckeyes. The nuts fall in autumn, lie dormant through winter, then sprout with the onset of spring rains. This longer "shelf-life" appears to be an adaptation to the climate of central California where most of the annual rainfall comes in late winter and early spring.

### Planting buckeyes
I don't give established plants any special care. I do take extra pains, however, to give transplants a good start. I try to plant them only when dormant, either in fall or winter here in Arkansas. Even container-grown plants will sometimes wilt and die if transplanted after leafing out. If you must plant a buckeye during the growing season, protect it from the sun and water it regularly. In general, additional irrigation the first season is a good idea. I also broadcast timed-release fertilizer after planting to speed establishment. And a thick layer of compost topped with fallen leaves, simulating the forest floor, will make a buckeye feel right at home. ☐

*Larry P. Lowman is the owner of Ridgecrest Nursery, which is located near Wynne, Arkansas.*

The California buckeye puts on a beautiful spring display, often under difficult circumstances. In its native range, it must make do on lean soil and endure extended dry spells.

The trailing flowers of pieris make a delicate springtime display. With its glossy, evergreen leaves, pieris is a refreshing addition to any partly shaded spot in the landscape, rewarding the gardener with much pleasure for little effort.

# In Praise of Pieris
## A spring-flowering evergreen shrub for shade

by Joyce Van Etten

Among broad-leaved evergreen shrubs, pieris is notable for its shade-tolerance and all-season interest. Its rich green, glossy foliage stands out year-round, and in early spring, a profusion of small, cup-shaped flowers, ranging from deep pink through cream to white, hangs in clusters like strings of beads. As a bonus, the flowers of some cultivars emit a light, fruity fragrance reminiscent of grape hyacinths. When the bronze-red new leaves appear, pieris assumes a soft, feathery look that can last as long as a month until the new leaves turn green. In winter, the flower buds, which range in color from green to dark red, look striking against the leaves. And pieris leaves don't curl in cold weather and look sorry as rhododendrons' do.

Also called andromeda, pieris is a medium-tall shrub that requires little care and can be grown from USDA Zones 4 to 8. Like other members of the heath family (*Ericaceae*), which includes rhododendrons and azaleas, pieris requires an acid pH, woodsy soil and a good mulch year-round.

My interest in pieris began six years ago when I became curator of the Brooklyn Botanic Garden's collection of plants in the heath family. My challenge—to create a beautiful, interesting and educational display with plants just from the heath family—was made easier by pieris.

## Landscape uses

Green all year and dense in habit, pieris makes an excellent informal screen, either by itself or combined with other broad-leaved evergreens such as hollies, mountain laurels or rhododendrons. Daffodils, lilies and other shade-tolerant flowers make a pleasing picture against a backdrop of pieris. A single pieris can be a good focus in a shady, secluded corner. For any garden that's lovingly tended and frequently toured, pieris show well under close inspection.

Here at the Botanic Garden, our pieris collection grows in the dappled shade of a gnarled old cork tree (Phellodendron amurense) and several oaks. I've combined pieris with a few of its later-blooming relatives, enkianthus and leucothoe, both white-flowered shrubs. Even during the "quiet" months from mid-summer through early fall, the graceful form of pieris creates a cool, serene feeling among the deep shadows of arching oaks. In winter, the red pieris buds create a warm feeling, and counting them gives a promise of spring.

### Pieris japonica

I'll describe most of the pieris I know. Of the six pieris species in cultivation, I grow four, along with ten cultivars and two interspecific hybrids (crosses between two species). Collectively, they bloom from late February until late April here in Zone 6.

One species, Pieris japonica, hardy from Zones 5 to 8, is very dependable for both northern and southern gardens and offers a host of excellent cultivars. Among the first cultivars of P. japonica to bloom, 'Valley Valentine' flowers here at the garden from late February through late March. This compact low-grower, which reaches about 3 ft. tall, bears a profusion of pink and white flowers that appear deep pink from a distance. Last year, on February 26, its bright pink flowers peeked out from under puffy caps of snow, but 'Valley Valentine', undaunted, bloomed on.

'Dorothy Wycoff' blooms around the same time as 'Valley Valentine'. Exceptionally glossy, dark green leaves contrast with very elegant white flowers. Its red-brown flower stems and calyxes (outer whorls of flower parts), silhouette the flower clusters and emphasize their graceful, drooping lines.

'Valley Rose' is another early bloomer, with pale pink flowers and a pleasing asymmetrical shape. 'Shojo',

Pieris is a versatile landscape plant and can be grown as an informal hedge, a single specimen, or combined with other shrubs, as in the entryway planting shown above.

## Andromeda (Pieris spp.)

pee-E-ris

- Spring-blooming, evergreen shrub with shiny, green foliage.

- Grows 3 ft. to 6 ft. tall.

- Hardy in USDA Zones 4-8, depending on species or cultivar.

- Bell-shaped flowers in clusters; pink, white or cream colors.

- Prefers part shade; needs acid, humus-rich soil.

- Needs regular watering until established.

- Plant as screen or specimen plant.

a very early blooming dwarf form with trails of medium pink flowers, is probably the most noticed pieris here. This 3-ft. tall shrub, with its half-size flower clusters, is ideal for a small garden. All four of the cultivars I've mentioned so far have particularly ornamental flower buds—tinted red in the fall and turning dark red in winter.

Other P. japonica cultivars begin blooming here around mid-March. My favorite of the group is a 30-year-old specimen of 'Bonsai'. Well-named for its Oriental look, it grows into a 5-ft.

tall, picturesque form with tiers of creamy white flowers. The dark green leaves of 'Crispa', so glossy that they almost seem unreal, are an excellent foil for its long clusters of white flowers, and their twisted shapes provide year-round interest. 'White Cascade' bears 5-in. long, white flower clusters that are longer and larger than those of other P. japonica cultivars. Its upright, mounded form is more regular than the shape of most cultivars. 'Yakusimana' is a mounded, foot-tall rock garden gem with a profusion of white flowers amid small leaves.

The bright red new leaves of 'Mountain Fire' provide a fiery display for several weeks, a striking highlight against the reddish and bronze new growth of other cultivars or shrubs. The flowers are white and less showy than those of other pieris, but this cultivar takes more sun and is generally more vigorous. 'Scarlet O'Hara', a similar cultivar, has showier flowers but does not hold its fiery color as long.

Several other cultivars of P. japonica are grown more for their leaves and form than for their flowers, which are rare or subtle, at best. 'Bisbee Dwarf', a 2-ft. tall, small-leaved plant with a regular, mounded shape and reddish new growth, makes a good substitute for a low boxwood hedge. 'Pygmaea', a low, twiggy mound 1 ft. to 2 ft. tall, has small, narrow leaves. I've successfully planted this interesting oddity as a low, informal edging; it also looks good in a rock garden. According to Long Island nurseryman

Photo: Susan Kahn; illustration: Rosalind Loeb Wanke

One of the earliest pieris to bloom, 'Valley Valentine' (above) is covered with luscious pink flowers for nearly a month. *Pieris taiwanensis* (below), with its pendulous white flower sprays, is best adapted to warmer regions in the South.

Jim Cross, 'Variegata', an eye-catching plant with white-edged leaves, tolerates a borderline Zones 4 and 5 climate. Its bronze-red new growth makes a charming contrast to the variegated older leaves. This one is a slow-grower.

## More pieris choices

The most cold-hardy species (Zones 4 to 6) is *P. floribunda*, a Northeast native that blooms here by the end of March. This good-looking, low plant, about 3 ft. wide by 4 ft. tall, has a pleasing, rather irregular, upright shape, well suited to rock gardens, woodlands and other informal settings. Its white flowers are held more upright than those of *P. japonica*, and the leaf is a lighter, less glossy, green. One cultivar, 'Millstream', has an exceptional white flower. *P. floribunda* performs poorly in the southern U.S. unless planted in cool areas of high elevation, in rocky, well-drained soil.

'Browers Beauty', a hybrid of *P. japonica* and *P. floribunda*, is hardy to Zone 4. This slow-growing pieris blooms fairly late, and its semi-pendant white flowers stay open for nearly a month. I've planted it next to 'Mountain Fire', whose red new growth makes a striking contrast with the white flowers.

The showiest species are *P. formosa* and *P. forrestii*, both with bright red new leaves and striking long white flower clusters. These species might be rated as winter-hardy to Zone 8, but they require cooler summers than those in Zone 8. They grow well only on the West Coast, from the State of Washington to San Francisco, where they are outstanding plants.

Happily, 'Forest Flame' and 'Valley Fire', hybrids of *P. japonica × forrestii*, are more widely adapted than *P. forrestii* alone. Both cultivars are hardy to Zone 6 and tolerate the summers of Zone 6 and Zone 7. In the middle of April, both are stars, creating a stunning effect with their lovely white flowers against bright red new growth. Here in Zone 6, because of our cold winters, they don't always flower, but I still consider them worth growing for the color of the new growth, which changes from bright red to pale red and yellow. Both hybrids need a little more shade than other pieris, as the new growth sunburns easily.

Other species are *P. taiwanensis* (Zones 7 to 8), which bears handsome, long white flower clusters, and *P. phillyreifolia* (Zone 6), a southeastern native vine with upright flowers, which blooms best with plenty of moisture.

In the future, you can expect to see new and improved pieris cultivars. Breeders around the world are working to develop pieris with larger and longer flower clusters, deeper pink and near-red flowers, more compact growth, smaller leaves, and resistance to lacebugs, a common pest.

## Culture

Pieris are excellent plants for part-shade. With few exceptions, they will grow well and flower heavily in sun, but on the East Coast, at least, lacebugs become much more troublesome on plants growing in full sun.

To provide the acidic, woods-like soil that pieris requires, I work 4 in. of peat into the top foot of soil when I plant. In humus-poor soils, add up to 6 in. of peat. Other organic materials, such as composted oak leaves or pine needles, also help loosen the soil.

In the South, with its heavy summer rains and warmer soils, you must provide excellent drainage to prevent waterlogging and avoid phytophthera, a fungus that causes root rot and can kill plants. To provide good drainage, J.C. Raulston, a plant physiologist at North Carolina State University, recommends planting pieris in raised beds of shredded pine bark, rather than peat, which disintegrates too quickly in warmer soils.

Pieris can be planted in spring or fall—April through May or September through October in Zone 6 and north, March or October farther south. After removing the plant from its pot, tease out about an inch of roots all around the rootball with your fingers or sharp pruners to encourage potbound roots to grow out into the surrounding soil. Pieris should be planted at the same depth they were growing in the pot. To allow for their mature size, space plants 6 ft. apart. (Dwarf cultivars can be planted closer.) For a more immediate effect, you can plant them as close as 3 ft. and later transplant them farther apart.

Water well the first year; I give my plants 1 in. to 1½ in. of water per week. Once the plants are established, irrigation is less crucial, but a thorough watering during summer dry periods is beneficial.

In the spring, I fertilize with a 10-6-4 formulation, applied at half rate. Proper soil preparation and an acidic mulch should prevent chlorosis, usually a symptom of iron deficiency that shows up as yellow leaves with only the veins remaining green. If you

The bright red new growth of pieris 'Mountain Fire' (above) creates a surprising show in late April, as impressive as another season of bloom. By autumn, the once-brilliant new growth of 'Forest Flame' (below) has mellowed to a warm orange and yellow glow.

suspect chlorosis, green-up your pieris by fertilizing in early spring with a formulation for acid-loving plants, or lower the pH more permanently with ferrous sulfate. (Pieris also seem to develop chlorosis more frequently if they're growing in full sun.)

On the East Coast, lacebugs occasionally can be a problem. The presence of these ⅛-in. long insects with clear lacy wings is indicated by dirty specks or smudges on the undersides of the leaves, which turn yellow and have a pinpricked appearance. Large numbers of these sap-sucking insects can wreak extensive damage. If you detect lacebugs early enough, Safers insecticidal soap checks them. For severe cases, spray with a systemic insecticide such as Orthene (acephate). Follow label directions and wear protective clothing. If you have a persistent lacebug problem, you might plant *P. floribunda*, a resistant species.

Since pieris are shallow-rooted, mulching is essential. In the fall, I rake whole oak leaves onto the beds to a depth of 6 in. You could also mulch with wood chips, pine needles or the like, spread to about 3 in. deep. Other than removing dead or broken limbs, it's not necessary to prune pieris, as the natural form is quite picturesque. □

## SOURCES

*The author recommends these mail-order suppliers, who offer one or more of the pieris mentioned in the article.*

**ForestFarm,** 990 Tetherow Road, Williams, OR 97544-9599. Catalog $3.

**Greer Gardens,** 1280 Goodpasture Island Road, Eugene, OR 97401-1794. 503-686-8266. Catalog $3.

**Roslyn Nursery,** 211 Burrs Lane, Dix Hills, NY 11746. 516-643-9347. Catalog $3.

**Siskiyou Rare Plant Nursery,** 2825 Cummings Road, Medford, OR 97501. 503-772-6846. Catalog $2, refundable with first order.

*Joyce Van Etten is curator of the heath-family collection at the Brooklyn Botanic Garden in Brooklyn, NY.*

'Complicata' bears flowers lovely in their simplicity, with showy yellow stamens that glow amid dark petals. This 7-ft.-tall shrub, like other Gallicas, blooms once in spring.

# Old Roses for the Small Garden

## A wealth of blooms from tough, hardy shrubs

by Dave Dunn

I love old roses for their hardiness, vigor, and huge variety of flower shapes and sizes. And I love them for their persistence among rose growers in spite of the overwhelming popularity of modern hybrids. My wife, Judy, and I grow as many as we can in the backyard of our home in New Britain, Connecticut. We've laid out large beds with grass paths between them in an area about 70 ft. by 80 ft. and planted more than 200 varieties of old roses. We maintain the roses under crowded conditions by careful planting and maintenance, by yearly pruning, and by choosing relatively small, tough varieties. Our rewards are a garden with symmetry, order, and diversity, but above all the chance to savor and enjoy a colorful, fragrant tapestry of flowers, especially at peak bloom in late spring.

When I say "old roses," I mean varieties that in looks and vigor resemble ancestral roses. Modern roses, especially the Hybrid Teas and Floribundas that dominate the nursery trade, are the result of crossing many species and varieties to achieve certain characteristics: new and vivid colors, continuous bloom, restrained growth, and many-petaled flowers. The old roses I grow are generally larger plants, with fragrant flowers and a wider range of flower shapes.

If you're new to old roses, I suggest that you simply grow a few plants and enjoy them before you try to sort out and master the daunting profusion of rose groups, species and varieties. Old roses divide into many groups, each with the same ancestral species or two in their parentage and a family resemblance among plants. The oldest roses, some in cultivation for 1,000 years and more, belong to the Gallica, Alba and Damask

---

### Old roses (*Rosa* species and hybrids)

- Thorny deciduous shrubs, with an enormous range of growth habits, from dwarfs to large climbers
- Flowers often highly fragrant; simple to showy
- Most cultivars flower about 3 weeks in spring; some rebloom in fall; a few bloom continuously in warm climates
- Full sun
- Slightly acid, well-drained soil
- Some cultivars hardy to Zone 3; many cultivars thrive in the South
- Use in shrub borders; on trellises; as hedges, edgings and specimens.

---

roses groups, whose varieties are nearly all strongly fragrant. Later groups include the Centifolia, Moss and China roses, which entered cultivation in Europe more than 200 years ago. Among more recent old roses, Portlands were the first to draw repeat-flowering from crosses with China roses, but were soon overtaken in popularity by two new repeat-flowering groups, the Bourbons and the Hybrid Perpetuals, developed in the last half of the 18th century. (For more about old-rose groups, see Resources on p. 34.)

Practically all of the old-rose groups are hardy here in northern Connecticut, where Zone 5 and Zone 6 merge, and many old roses thrive in Zone 3 and Zone 4. Few modern types are as hardy—most require considerable winter protection in Zone 5.

**Old roses offer a wealth of color on hardy bushes that can be trained to small spaces.**

Photos, except as noted: Staff; illustration: Rosalind L. Wanke

We can grow Gallicas, Damasks, Centifolias, Mosses, Portlands, Albas, Bourbons, and some Perpetuals, both species and hybrids. The old roses include three fairly tender groups—Teas, Chinas and Noisettes (see "Old roses that take the heat" on p. 35)—but you can find a few hardy varieties in all three groups. For example, I have two massive plants of 'Sombreuil', a Tea with double white flowers.

Despite the long-standing notion that all old roses are one-time bloomers, about half of our 200 varieties are recurrent or repeat bloomers: the plants flower heavily in spring, rest about two months, and then make new growth and rebloom from late summer through fall. It's true that many old roses flower for only three weeks, but they make up for the brevity of their season by the sheer number of their blossoms.

I delight in the history of old roses, and am fascinated by the fact that 'Maxima', a white rose from the 2,000-year-old Alba group, was grown by the Romans; that 'Rosa Mundi', one of the Gallica roses (a group grown in Europe from the 12th century on), may have been named by Henry II of England for his mistress, Rosamund; and that 'Autumn Damask', prob-

ably brought to Europe by the Crusaders, was the first continuously flowering variety known in the West until China roses made their debut in the Empress Josephine's Malmaison garden during Napoleon's reign.

## Outstanding old rose varieties

While there are literally hundreds of old garden roses, some set the standard of

Pure white and semi-double, the flower of 'Nastarana' is highly fragrant. A Noisette rose, 'Nastarana' blooms heavily on a 2-ft. to 4-ft. plant.

excellence and belong in any old rose garden. I think first of the 1840 Gallica, 'Cardinal de Richelieu', which is extremely hardy. Gallicas are short and spreading plants, with riotous colors. The flowers of the 'Cardinal' start out a rich royal purple, then turn deep blue. They offer effective contrasts and harmonies when planted among other cultivars.

One of the finest white roses of all time is the Damask 'Madame Hardy', first cultivated in 1832. It's striking in the garden, producing clumps of bloom. The white, very full flowers are popular at rose shows, and often win Dowager Queen, the award given to the best flower from an old rose variety introduced before 1867.

Among the most dazzling flowers in my garden is 'Rosa Mundi', a richly fragrant Gallica with light pink petals streaked wildly with dark pink. (You can see it on the facing page.) The 4-ft.-tall plants are healthy and flower prolifically in spring. Two other eye-catching flowers are 'Fantin-Latour' and 'The Bishop', both Centifolias, with a profusion of petals but very different appearance. The billowing light pink petals of 'Fantin-Latour' crowd and swirl together, while the magenta-to-purple petals of 'The Bishop' overlap in neat tiers.

I've learned over the years to appreciate the beauty of simple rose flowers, which are those with only five petals. My favorite is the Swamp rose (*Rosa palustris*), a species that I first saw growing wild on the roadside and immediately loved. The plant tolerates adverse conditions, and the spreading flowers are pink. I also recommend 'Complicata', a Gallica with bright yellow stamens that stand out against dark petals, and 'Mermaid', a climbing rose known for its creamy yellow-to-white petals and prominent sulphur-yellow stamens. 'Mermaid' is almost evergreen, and blooms continuously. It's marginally hardy here, but I continue to grow it for its regal form and rare color.

## Soil preparation and planting

Roses need fertile, well-drained soil and at least six hours of sunlight a day. When I started, my backyard was deeply shrouded in shade, and the soil was poor and too acid (pH 4.5 to 5.0). First, I let in the sun by hiring an arborist to take down trees. Though many trees remain, my roses now get six to ten hours of sunlight a day. Then I rebuilt the soil. With help from my three teenage sons, I cleared the beds of rocks and tree roots, and mixed dozens of bags of topsoil, peat moss and composted manure into the soil, along with hundreds of pounds of ground limestone to raise the pH. Roses prefer slightly acid soil; anywhere in the range of pH 6.0 to 6.5 is considered suitable.

It pays to plant with care. Most mail-order roses are year-old plants, shipped bare-root. They consist of a few cut-back

A profusion of tightly overlapping petals glistens with dew on a flower of 'The Bishop', a 5-ft.-tall shrub that blooms prolifically in early summer.

branches and a few woody roots, and they need cosseting to get a good start.

The keys to planting are speed, good soil and water. From the moment a plant arrives, keep the roots moist, and set it in the ground as soon as you can. Dig a broad hole—plenty of loose soil encourages root growth the first year. I make 2-ft.-square holes that are deep enough so that I can place the graft union (where the desired variety joins the rootstock) at ground level. When I finish digging a hole, I sprinkle a cup of bone meal in it to provide phosphorus and a bit of nitrogen. I wet the soil thoroughly before planting. Usually I fill the hole and then let it drain. Next I set the plant in place and fill the hole with a 50-50 mix of soil and decomposed organic matter—compost, leaf mold or composted cow manure. As I fill the hole, I water to help settle soil around the roots.

Like all newly-set-out bare-root plants, roses need regular watering. I water daily until the plants have sent out new branches and made at least 1 ft. of growth. Then I water them whenever I water established plants.

## Maintaining old roses

All roses need constant attention to do their best. Though many old roses are tougher than modern types, with more tolerance for drought, cold and other adverse conditions, they're nonetheless susceptible to diseases and insects. Inspect the garden regularly and catch problems early.

Make sure roses have adequate moisture. I water whenever rainfall is short, making sure the plants have an inch of water a week. Avoid sprinklers, since they wet the foliage and encourage fungal diseases. I use soaker hoses, but drip tape would work, too. My soaker hoses are all linked, so I can water all the plants at once, which is a great convenience.

I fertilize the plants frequently and enrich the soil with organic matter every year. In late March, when buds green up and swell, I spread a cup of 10-10-10 fertilizer and a spadeful of composted cow manure around each shrub, and work the amendments shallowly into the soil. I continue to fertilize each plant during the growing season, with one cup of 10-10-10 a month, and then stop in September to let the plants slow their growth and develop hardiness for the winter. I water each plant every two to three weeks with a gallon of fish emulsion solution to provide trace elements. I test the soil pH every spring and spread lime if the pH is below 6.0.

Mulch is a great help in growing roses. It eliminates weeds, helps moderate soil temperatures and slows evaporation of water from the soil. I mulch all my plants with 3 in. of finely shredded cedar

The large, billowing, light pink flowers of 'Fantin-Latour' (above) have a delicate, pleasing fragrance. This broad, 5-ft. shrub blooms in spring. Streaked and flecked, the 3-in. flowers of 'Rosa Mundi' (below) are among the boldest of old roses. They are heavily fragrant, and grow on a 4-ft. plant.

Shoup has adopted an old technique called pegging for some varieties, using wire staples to anchor canes to the ground (below). Pegging arranges the canes like the spokes of a wheel and gives the plant an arching shape (above). The horizontal position of the canes prompts lateral buds to break, multiplying shoots and flowers.

ways. We hammer staples into wooden fences, posts and trellises, and fasten the canes to them with twist-ties, leaving slack. As the canes grow, we untwist and replace the ties to avoid girdling. If we miss a tie, it usually rusts apart before harming the cane. We add ties whenever the new growth is long enough to train. We also train roses on wire trellises, fastening the canes at intervals with twist-ties, and on walls, tying the canes to wires or staples.

I made a mistake with 'Celine Forestier' (1,2,4,9), a Noisette that turned out to have stiff canes. I planted it by a low fence, with the intention of working it through the palings, but found that the canes resisted being bent and would break if forced. This pretty yellow rose with a green button eye would be more appropriately used with its canes fanned out against a wall or a trellis.

I found that the Hybrid Musk class contains a number of good climbers, too. Hybrid Musks, developed in England, are hardier than are the Noisettes. They include varieties that form gracefully arched bushes 3 ft. to 5 ft. in height and as much as 7 ft. across. Stunning specimens on their own, they also make attractive landscape accents when combined with other ornamentals. In addition, varieties this size can be trained to a trellis with good effect. We have two plants of a Hybrid Musk called 'Cornelia' (1,2,3,4,7,9,10) in the garden. Introduced in 1925, 'Cornelia' has small, double, salmon-pink flowers that open in great profusion from bright coral buds.

One plant is growing as a lush, fountaining bush. The other is trained on wires that run from the base to the top of an arbor, making a fan 8 ft. wide.

For training some varieties, I've had good luck with an old English landscaping technique called pegging, in which canes are fastened to the ground at their tips, lowering and rounding the plant's silhouette and increasing its spread. In 1987, when one of my staff pegged several Bourbon and Hybrid Perpetual roses, we not only liked the new shape, but also found that pegging multiplied flower production. Anytime a rose cane is bent to

the side, new growth springs from its lateral buds and reaches up for the sun. On a pegged rose, the number of canes increases many times and the number of flowers increases tenfold.

Not all roses are suited to pegging. Well-branched, shrubby bushes are obviously unsuitable, as they lack the necessary long, graceful canes. Climbing roses are also out of the running, because their canes get too long and untidy. The perfect rose is one with flexible canes in the 5-ft. to 7-ft. range, one that might make a lax, ungraceful shrub if left alone. If I had to choose a pegging rose, it would be 'Madame Isaac Pereire' (1,2,3,4,6,9,10), a Bourbon introduced in 1881 (top photo). It's a perfect size, with easily trained 5-ft. canes, and it produces big, richly scented flowers of a deep rose-madder for up to three months straight in the spring, with some repeat flowering in the fall. Bourbon roses are moderately hardy. If you want to experiment with pegging in the North, you might try the extremely cold-hardy Hybrid Perpetual roses.

Pegging involves a few simple steps. New canes are fragile, so we let a plant grow unhampered for the first year. At the start of the second year, we cut back any canes that are longer than their neighbors, pinch off the last few buds on the rest to discourage them from growing longer, and then peg the canes, trying to space them evenly like spokes on a wheel. To hold the tips of the canes in place in our windy location, we use 5-in.-long staples made from 12-gauge galva-

Photos: top, Michael Shoup, Jr.; bottom, Staff

nized wire. (Coat-hanger wire would work, too.) A pegged cane occasionally takes root and produces tip growth. If this happens, it's easy enough to pull it up, trim away the unwanted growth and re-peg the cane. New canes that arise from the base of the plant have to grow and harden before they can be pegged.

### Finding your own

I encourage you to seek out and collect your own old roses. You might save a variety on the verge of oblivion. We've gone back to old collecting sites and found the original plants bulldozed. A good way to start is to follow up on casual comments such as, "My grandmother planted this rose out in back of the house, and it blooms all the time and we never do a thing to it." You can also prospect in likely spots, among them cemeteries that predate 1900 and fence rows of long-abandoned farmhouses. I know enthusiasts who like to call themselves "Rose Rustlers" and joke about getting shot for trespassing, but in fact when they find old roses, they ask permission to take cuttings and usually are welcome.

The time to look for old roses and take cuttings is in the late spring to early summer, when the once-blooming varieties are in flower, or in the fall, when ever-blooming types are at their best. Cuttings taken at these times, when the plants are in a flush of growth, are more likely to root than are cuttings taken at other times.

For cuttings, choose canes that are neither old nor new. They should be this season's growth, but not so young that they're tender and weak. To judge, look at the top foot or two of a cane. When you find a suitable cane, nip off and discard the succulent first few inches, then cut the rest into 3-in. pieces, each with three buds. Pull off the bottom leaf so that you have an inch of bare cane to stick in a pot. If the cutting has flowers, cut them off. If you have to transport cuttings any distance, they'll travel well wrapped in slightly damp newspaper in an open box or plastic bag. We've had people drive overnight from Louisiana with cuttings that arrived in excellent shape.

When you get home, stick each cutting in a damp, but not wet, rooting medium. As I mentioned earlier, I use highly decomposed pine bark, mixed with perlite and a little sand. A similar mix, with peat moss instead of pine bark, or any light, well-drained potting soil should be fine. You can dust the base of the cutting with rooting hormone before planting, but many roses root so readily that it makes no discernible difference.

Until the cuttings can put down roots, they'll be getting all their moisture from the air, so they need a humid environment. Cover them with a glass jar, a cut-up plastic milk jug, or anything else that will produce a greenhouse effect. Make sure they don't get too much direct sun, so they don't boil, and lift the cover now and then to be sure they don't rot from too much moisture. When your cuttings begin to sprout new leaves, in six to eight weeks, they are rooted and ready to be gradually introduced to direct sunlight and then planted where you want them to go. Before we set out new plants, we prepare the soil by tilling-in decomposed pine bark— about 50-50 soil and bark by volume.

If this seems too technical, please remember that many early cottage gardeners just pruned their roses in the spring and stuck the cuttings right in the ground, and had pretty fair success.

Some old roses are difficult to propagate. I've had a lot of trouble rooting 'Maréchal Niel' (1,3,4,5,6,7,8,9), a Noisette climber with fat, fragrant yellow flowers, widely grown in the South after its introduction in 1864. A true antique, it is the rose most often mentioned by our customers as the one their grandmothers grew and loved. Unfortunately, 'Maréchal Niel' has changed over the years from one of the most vigorous of roses to one of the least vigorous, possibly because of a viral infection that has weakened all the available stock. It's nearly impossible to get cuttings to root well by any method I've tried, and I've never been able to produce a successful crop. I've also struggled with the short, thorny and rather unattractive shrub rose named 'Harison's Yellow' (1), which is commonly thought of as the Yellow Rose of Texas (though we all know that the true Yellow Rose was a woman). This year, I finally propagated it by heel divisions—taking portions of the plant base with roots attached to start new plants. This is more time-consuming than propagation with cuttings, and requires extra stock bushes, since it takes more material, but now I have a small crop.

### Favorites

When I'm asked to say which is my favorite old rose, I often name the 'Duchesse de Brabant' (1,3,4,10). This Tea rose from 1857 has one of the most attractive bushes I've seen, about 4 ft. high, rounded and graceful, with full, light-green, slightly wavy foliage. It's almost constantly in bloom, with cupped pink flowers that demonstrate the distinctive Tea fragrance to perfection and are beautiful in cut-flower arrangements. It's a rose I like to see people buy, because I know that once they've grown it, they'll be back for more old roses. Deep down in my heart, though, I have to admit that 'Mermaid', the wild climber, will always be the most special to me. It was the first, after all, and I captured it myself. □

---

*Michael Shoup, Jr.'s business, The Antique Rose Emporium, is in Brenham, Texas.*

Shoup has found that most old roses root readily from cuttings, but not 'Maréchal Niel', a Noisette climber once widely grown in the South. Although he uses a mist chamber and rooting hormones, he has been unable to produce a crop of this variety.

For cuttings, Shoup chooses a cane of the current season, old enough to be stiff. He discards the tender tip and then makes three-bud cuttings (above). Before a cutting goes in potting soil, he removes the bottommost leaf (below), taking care to preserve the axillary bud, which will sprout if the top two buds die.

Miniature roses come in a range of sizes and growth forms. The clear-pink flowers of the climber 'Jeanne Lajoie' are only about 1¼ in. in diameter, but they're much larger than any single blossom of the bush mini 'Popcorn', clustered below them.

The miniature ground cover 'Nozomi' in Lowe's rock garden is shown here early in its first blooming period. Later the flowers will lose their pink tinge and make a carpet of white.

and for lack of another spot, I planted them there, planning to move them to the greenhouse in the fall. I never got around to it, and much to my surprise, despite being unprotected for the winter and flooded in the spring, 35 of the minis survived *and* did better than any of the other roses in our garden.

Today this bed contains 150 minis, mostly large colorful clusters of 'My Valentine', 'Seabreeze', 'Lavender Jewel' and 'Debbie', intermingled with polyantha roses and miniature-rose trees. At the end of the bed is one of my favorite miniatures, 'Nozomi', a large plant with profuse thumbnail-size white flowers. It's sold as a miniature climber, but I think of it as a large ground cover.

In front of the house, bordering the street and the adjacent property, is an *L*-shaped bed containing my collection of Portland and modern shrub roses. A number of bush minis edge this bed, including 'My Valentine', which, if you haven't guessed by now, is my favorite mini. It's about 18 in. high and disease-resistant, and nothing puts out better sprays. A single stem can have 20 blooms; a row of plants, thousands of little deep-red flowers. It's an ideal border plant: not too tall, flowers abundantly and repeats well.

A large terraced rock garden borders the driveway. There we grow dwarf pinks, sedums and cacti with miniature roses and dwarf evergreens. Many of the more formal miniatures (that is, those with high-centered flowers) work well here: 'Cupcake', 'Minnie Pearl', 'Anita Charles' and 'Black Jade', anchored by large plants of 'Anytime' and 'Nozomi'. The predominant miniature in this garden is 'Rainbow's End', for my money the best all-around miniature. A bush mini, about 15 in. high, it's ideal for borders and rock gardens, and shows lovely color and form, though it seldom has more than four flowers per stem. The rock garden is always changing, and last year at the foot of a lamp post, we planted 60 sq. ft. of the white-flowered miniature 'Snow Carpet' underplanted with 400 blue and yellow species crocuses.

**Planting**

Like all roses, miniatures do best in rich, well-drained soil. We build our rose beds by mixing loam and cow manure, about two parts to one, with lime and bone meal. Our beds are as much as 30 in. deep, but if your bed is just for minis, 15 in. deep will do. We put down a 6-in. layer of mixed loam and manure, rototill in a healthy dusting of lime and bone meal, then add more layers. The lime raises the pH of our acid soil to between 6 and 7, the range roses prefer. The bone meal provides phosphorous to promote rooting and flowering. If you're planting individual minis, fill each 15-in.-deep

Photo, bottom: Mike Lowe

As edging for a garden bed, miniature bush roses can provide more variety and interest than marigolds or impatiens—and they're perennial. Two of Lowe's favorites are 'My Valentine', on the left, and 'Rainbow's End', on the right.

## A miniature history

Descendants of *Rosa chinensis* 'Minima', miniature roses made their way from China to Europe sometime before 1800. One of the earliest records I've found is the illustrations of miniatures in Harry C. Andrews' *A Monograph of the Genus Rosa,* published in 1805. By the mid-19th century, miniatures had become popular pot plants. Thirty years later, however, they had all but disappeared from the books, victims of fashion perhaps, their hardiness and potential as garden plants as yet unknown.

Miniatures were rediscovered in 1917, by one Colonel Roulet, a Frenchman, who found one growing in a window box in a Swiss village. Named *Rosa Roulettii* in the Colonel's honor, this rose was soon sold on a wide scale by his friend, Henri Correvon. Though the hybridizing of roses began in the 1880s, the first commercially significant hybridizing of miniatures occurred in the 1930s, when a Dutchman, Jan de Vink, crossed miniatures with hybrid teas and floribundas. The miniature gene being dominant, most of the offspring were miniature. The best of the hybrids of the 1930s and 1940s were those of a Spaniard, Pedro Dot, whose 'Baby Gold Star' is still sold today.

Miniatures continued to be thought of as pot plants until Ralph S. Moore of Visalia, California, began hybridizing them in the 1950s. Moore crossed minis with many other types of roses, creating miniature ground covers, climbers and bush roses, all suitable for the garden, as well as miniature flowers in a wide variety of colors and forms. By the 1970s, Moore had been joined by other hybridizers, professional and amateur, and miniatures began to sell in big numbers. In 1987, three million miniatures were sold in the United States, triple the number sold each year from 1950 to 1975.

Relatively easy to hybridize, many new varieties of miniatures are offered every year. Because minis are also easy to propagate and grow, there are far more commercial growers of them than of full-size roses. This widespread hybridizing and vigorous commercial competition has revolutionized the rose world, and made it hard for mini lovers to keep up. I used to grow all the new varieties each year, but recently I've fallen way behind. There are just too many out there.   —*M.L.*

Shown in September, at the height of its second bloom, 'Seabreeze' (above) demonstrates the virtues of minis: abundant bloom throughout the season on a compact plant. 'Seabreeze' is a large bush mini, growing to 24 in. in Lowe's garden. Like other vigorous growers, it would require pruning to maintain that height if grown farther south.

Miniature roses, like their full-size relations, offer lovely blossoms across a range of colors. These examples, photographed in Lowe's garden during the plants' second blooming period, are 'Debbie' (top left), 'Black Jade' (above left) and 'Radiant' (above right).

## SOME MINIATURE-ROSE VARIETIES

| Name | Height (H); spread (S) | Flower form[1]; color | Source[2] | Comments |
|---|---|---|---|---|
| **BUSH** | | | | |
| 'Black Jade' | 12-15 in. (H) | HT; dark red | 2,4,7,8,9,10 | Good cut flower; a show rose. |
| 'Debbie' | 2-4 ft. (H) | OP; orange-yellow blend | 4 | Low hedge-type rose. |
| 'Debut' | 12-15 in. (H) | OP; white with pink edges | 7 | Edging plant; informal bloom; 1988 AA winner. |
| 'Green Ice' | 10-15 in. (H) | Rosette clusters; greenish white | 2,4,7,8,9,10 | Great sprays; good in borders. |
| 'Heavenly Days' | 18-24 in. (H) | HT; shades of light orange | 6,7 | Good clusters. |
| 'Lavender Jewel' | 15-18 in. (H) | HT, double; lavender | 2,4,7,8,9,10 | Best of double lavenders. |
| 'Little Eskimo' | 10-12 in. (H) | Rosette clusters; white-centered, touched with apricot | 4,9 | Great sprays; excellent in border. |
| 'Mossy Gem' (moss) | 10-12 in. (H); 24 in. (S) | OP; hot lavender-pink | 2 | Excellent low-growing and spreading plant. |
| 'My Valentine' | 18 in. (H) | OP, rosette clusters; deep red | 4 | Disease-resistant; wonderful sprays of flowers. |
| 'New Beginning' | 15-18 in. (H) | High-centered; shades of light to medium orange | 2,7 | Border plant; more formal bloom; 1988 AA winner. |
| 'Orange Sunblaze' | 20 in. (H) | OP; deep orange | 8,9 | Good border plant; lots of flowers. |
| 'Party Girl' | 18-24 in. (H) | HT; peach | 4,7,8,10 | Clusters of three; fragrant. |
| 'Popcorn' | 12-15 in. (H) | Single; white | 4,6,7,10 | Clusters of thirty to forty ½-in. blooms. |
| 'Radiant' | 5 ft. (H) | HT; clear orange-red | 6,7 | A pillar-type rose. |
| 'Rainbow's End' | 15 in. (H) | HT, double; yellow-red | 4,6,7,8,9,10 | Ideal border plant; good cut flower. |
| 'Rosa Roulettii' | 15-18 in. (H) | Loose double; lilac-pink | 1,3 | The original Colonel Roulet mini. |
| 'Seabreeze' | 24 in. (H) | Cupped double; light pink | 10 | Makes a lovely low hedge. |
| 'Simplex' | 15-18 in. (H) | Single; white | 2,4,6,7,8 | Simple but outstanding. |
| 'Sweet Chariot' | 10 in. (H); 24 in. (S) | OP, rosette clusters; lavender-pink | 2,4,6,8,9 | Also good as ground cover and in hanging baskets. |
| **CLIMBERS** | | | | |
| 'Jeanne Lajoie' | 4½-12 ft. (H) | HT, double; pink | 2,4,6,7 | Best climbing mini; abundant bloom. |
| 'Little Girl' | 4-6 ft. (H) | HT, double; bright pink | 4,8 | A pillar-type rose; excellent cut flower. |
| **GROUND COVERS** | | | | |
| 'Nozomi' | 15 in. (H); 4 ft. (S) | OP, single; white | 5 | Mounds, then sprawls. |
| 'Snow Carpet' | 2 in. (H); 2 ft. (S) | OP, single; white | 4,8 | Ground-hugging; excellent as a cover plant for bulbs. |

[1] HT = hybrid tea; OP = open, flat, many-petaled.
[2] Sources are keyed to the companies listed in the box at right.

*NOTE: Height and spread are not exact; all but AA winners are based on performance in author's New Hampshire garden. Different climate and growing conditions will produce different results.*

planting hole with loam and manure or compost, adding ¼ cup of bone meal and, if necessary, lime.

Miniatures are sold potted or bare-root; most sold in the United States are on their own roots, and I've found them to be hardier than grafted plants. Bare-root plants will be about 18 months old, so they're bigger and more expensive than potted plants, which usually are about five months old and come in small pots. By the second year in the garden, though, both plants will be about the same size.

Minis do far better when transplanted in the spring so that they can establish healthy root systems before cold weather. In the friable soil of our rose beds, the planting hole needs to be just big enough for the plant—a bulb planter works well for the potted minis we plant. I mix a tablespoon of Osmocote timed-release fertilizer (14-14-14) with the soil at the bottom of the hole to give the plant a good start in the first year. I may plant 100 minis at a time, so I don't bother to unwind bound roots, but the plants do well. I bury the bottom set of leaves on a potted mini; these plants tend to push out of the ground as they grow, and this gets them anchored firmly at the start.

## SOURCES

1. **The Antique Rose Emporium**, Rt. 5, Box 143, Brenham, TX 77833. Catalog $3.00.

2. **Gloria Dei Nursery**, 36 East Rd., High Falls Park, High Falls, NY 12440. Catalog free.

3. **Heritage Rose Gardens**, 16831 Mitchell Creek Dr., Fort Bragg, CA 95437. Catalog $1.00.

4. **Justice Miniature Roses**, 5947 S.W. Kahle Rd., Wilsonville, OR 97070. Catalog free.

5. **Lowe's Own-Root Rose Nursery**, 6 Sheffield Rd., Nashua, NH 03062. Catalog $2.00.

6. **Mini-Roses**, P.O. Box 4255, Station A, Dallas, TX 75208. Catalog free.

7. **Nor'East Miniature Roses, Inc.**, 58 Hammond St., Rowley, MA 01969. Catalog free.

8. **Oregon Miniature Roses, Inc.**, 8285 S.W. 185th Ave., Beaverton, OR 97007. Catalog free.

9. **Sequoia Nursery/Moore Miniature Roses**, 2519 East Noble Ave., Visalia, CA 93277. Catalog free.

10. **Springwood Miniature Roses**, RR #3, Caledon East, Ontario L0N 1E0, Canada. Canadian shipments only. Catalog $1.00.

*For an extensive listing of miniatures (and other roses) and rose suppliers, consult Beverly Dobson's* **Combined Rose List.** *Updated yearly, it's available for $11.50 postpaid from her at 215 Harriman Rd., Irvington, NY 10533.*

## Care

It's possible to grow minis successfully with very little care. I grew my first minis in 15-in.-deep holes filled with peat moss and loam. I filled a 5-gal. bucket with water and added two tablespoons of Joy dishwashing soap to control mites and one tablespoon of Rapid Grow to boost growth, and doused each of my five plants with this twice a week. They grew wonderfully.

Now that I grow so many miniatures, I do more to keep them all in good health. Roses are very heavy feeders, so I fertilize three or four times a season. I dig in Osmocote around the plants in spring as soon as the ground can be worked. About a week and a half before they bloom, I add a liquid rose fertilizer called Avant by siphoning it into my drip-irrigation system. (Avant, a 10-10-10 fertilizer with trace elements, is available for $19.75/gal. from Avant Horticultural Products, P.O. Box 15233, West Palm Beach, FL 33416; 800-334-7979; 800-226-7979 within Florida.) Between bloom periods, I toss a handful or two of 10-10-10 or 10-5-5 garden fertilizer at each plant. I also add fertilizer anytime I think a plant needs it — if it doesn't look good or lacks vigor. Sometime from the end of August to mid-September, I spray a dilute solution of Rapid Grow, ½ tablespoon per gallon of water, to boost the second bloom. I don't use stronger, longer-lasting granular fertilizers after about August 10 because I don't want the plants to overgrow right before frost. In all, I probably use a ton of 10-10-10 a year on all my roses. But I think that the main reason the plants are healthy is the five pickup-truck loads of well-rotted cow manure I topdress the beds with in the fall and early spring.

Minis should never be allowed to dry out, even during the winter. Because of their shallower root systems, miniatures need watering even more frequently than large roses do. If I could, I'd give each of my minis ½ gal. to 1 gal. of water each day. But they do okay on about half that. I've found that sprinklers set low to the ground or drip irrigation works better than overhead watering, because more water goes where the plants can use it.

**Pest and disease control** — When they're grown apart from other roses, miniatures tend to be less susceptible to most diseases and pests than standard roses are. Because I grow minis with my other roses, they're prey to the fungal diseases black spot and mildew, and to spider mites, aphids and Japanese beetles. To control these, I spray every 21 days with long-acting pesticides. But there are alternatives if you're growing fewer roses than I am.

Minis suffer in particular from spider mites, and the hotter and drier it is, the worse the problem. The first line of defense is a clean garden. Several times

Lowe prunes his minis in the spring. Because of their size, minis are less of a chore to prune than are most other roses.

during the summer, I blow all the debris from under the plants with a hand-held blower (reversing a vacuum cleaner will work, too). I've used a variety of pesticides to control mites, and I try to alternate them because the mites seem to develop a resistance if just one is used. Small infestations can be controlled by spraying the foliage — top and underside — with soapy water at three-day intervals (the length of the mite's reproductive cycle in hot weather). Spray in the morning to lessen the chance of fungal disease. This practice will help control aphids, too.

Most minis don't develop mildew, but a combination of hot days and cool nights will bring it on. Some minis are prone to black spot, especially late in the season or if it's been rainy. During these conditions, I spray a preventive fungicide such as Funginex. If mildew appears, I add benlate to the Funginex. It takes the spores of both fungal diseases about six hours to develop on a wet surface, so it's best to water early in the day so that the leaves can dry off. Paying attention to the weather and watering carefully can greatly reduce the plants' susceptibility to fungal diseases.

Japanese beetles are very difficult to control. I apply the pesticide oftanol in early spring to kill the grubs and therefore lessen damage caused by the adults later. If that doesn't work, I say the heck with it and suffer through the damage they cause.

Because most people know minis as potted plants, they believe that minis are tender. But almost all are hardier than

hybrid tea, floribunda and climbing roses, and most are even hardier than modern shrub roses. I seldom winter-protect my miniatures and they do extremely well, despite winter lows of -30°F. (The biggest rose killer is late-winter cold and wind coming when the sap is rising in the plants.) If I want more bloom or a bigger plant, however, I'll cover them, either with a Styrofoam rose cone or a wrapping of Microfoam (available at many nurseries). I protect them after there's at least 2 in. of frost in the ground, and remove the cones or wrappings about a month before the last frost.

## Pruning

Pruning minis can be as simple as removing the dead wood in the spring. I prune when the forsythias bloom — about a month to a month and a half before the last frost. During a really cold winter, the plants may die back near the ground, but usually I just need to trim a 15-in.-high bush about halfway back, cutting to the outside-facing buds so that the new growth is away from the center of the plant. You can determine how far back a cane has died by scratching its surface — if it's green underneath, it's alive.

You can also prune to control the height and shape of a plant. I'll do this anytime except late in the growing season, when I don't want the plants putting out new growth. I remove large old canes to give others room to grow. I normally just prune the dead wood out of ground covers and don't try to control the shape, but once in a while I go in and whack a plant back almost to the ground to keep it from taking over. You can prune climbers to any size you want. After the first bloom, I sometimes cut out some canes with dead bloom to encourage more second bloom.

I seal cuts on canes larger than ¼ in. to prevent cutter bees from boring into the freshly pruned wood and damaging the plant. I use Elmer's glue as a sealant. It dries clear, so I mix it with a little green food coloring to let me know which cuts I've sealed. I prefer glue to commercial tar-based preparations, which make the canes die back.

It's an exciting time for miniature-rose enthusiasts such as myself. Every year the hybridizers push into new territory. And they haven't even begun to experiment with new techniques. I look forward to the day, let's say 30 years from now, when, thanks to gene splicing, I'll be able to grow my entire collection of old garden and shrub roses as miniatures on a plot an 80-year-old can manage. □

*Mike Lowe lives in Nashua, New Hampshire. He runs Lowe's Own-Root Rose Nursery in addition to being a microwave engineer for Raytheon.*

# Rosa Rubrifolia

## Grow this rose for its multicolored foliage

by Martin Ray

In a family of beauty queens, *Rosa rubrifolia* offers mystery and subtlety, winning a place in the garden as much for its enhancement of companions as for its own good looks. *Rosa rubrifolia* is a shrub unadorned by fancy flowers or evocative names. It comes to gardens as a species, unexaggerated and unimproved.

The foliage of this plant is remarkable. In different lights and seasons, the leaves seem to combine purple, pink, blue and green, and from a distance they take on a silvery cast. "Rubrifolia" refers to the reddish-purple veins and margins of the leaves. Some authorities say that the correct name, because it was published first, is *Rosa glauca*, which describes the bluish hue of the leaf surface. Whatever the name (you'll find it both ways in catalogs), the coloration of the leaves is unique. No wonder this plant is so highly prized by flower arrangers in search of alternatives to the standard "greens."

*Rosa rubrifolia* is a widely adapted, 6-ft. to 8-ft. tall shrub native to the mountains of central and southern Europe. In North America it thrives as far north as USDA Zone 2, where winter lows may dip to -50°F. It also performs well in warmer areas, though I've heard that it languishes in Zones 8 through 10, either because of summer heat and humidity or because of mild winters.

### Year-round interest

I think of *Rosa rubrifolia* above all as a foliage plant, but beautiful leaves aren't all that it has to offer. Over a two- to three-week period in late spring (usually in June here in Massachusetts), a profusion of single, soft pink, 2-in.

## Rosa rubrifolia

- A species rose grown primarily for its colorful foliage, which is valued by flower arrangers.
- Hardy to USDA Zone 2; will perform well in warmer climates except Zones 8-10.
- Shrub form; grows 6 ft. to 8 ft. tall.
- Single, pink flowers measuring 2 in. across open over two- to three-week period in late spring.
- Red hips are ornamental in fall and attract birds.
- Largely pest- and disease-free.

wide flowers appears, forming clusters close to the stems. Although this display isn't likely to merit a star on your calendar of garden spectacles, the flowers do add a warm luster to the shrub's canopy, blending modestly with the foliage.

By September, the flowers have evolved into decorative fruits, the hips, which are as ornamental as the bloom and remain so over a much longer season. This isn't surprising considering that the rose family (*Rosaceae*) includes such beautiful fruits as cherries, apples and strawberries. The clusters of hips on *Rosa rubrifolia* resemble miniature persimmons in shape and color. By midwinter, they begin to shrivel and darken, drawing mild interest from chickadees, titmice and mockingbirds. The most regular nibbler on my plants is the cardinal, whose brows-

ing isn't thorough enough to prevent the appearance of seedlings at the base of the shrub in warm weather.

Even in the dormant season, *Rosa rubrifolia* enlivens the garden. Just outside my window the shrub's bare branches glow with a cinnamon color in the dull, winter landscape. At their tips, yellowed leaves droop like flags in the rigging of a becalmed yacht, awaiting a freshening breeze.

### Landscape use

I first encountered *Rosa rubrifolia* in the book *The Education of a Gardener* by English landscape architect Russell Page. He used the plant enthusiastically as a foliage shrub in plantings on the European continent. I've had great success with this shrub here in coastal Massachusetts. I particularly like it near the sea where its leaves evoke hues of water and sky in the garden. Despite exposure to stiff winds and occasional salt spray, the rose goes right on "rubrifoliating."

This plant can take on landscape roles as diverse as its own appearance. Think of it primarily as a moderator, blending colors from soft to strident, and harmonizing diverse shapes with its fine-textured foliage and rounded form. I find that *Rosa rubrifolia* combines most elegantly with companions that bear flowers or leaves in the red, blue or white range, colors that echo *R. rubrifolia's* own. Try it with such shrubs as red-leaf varieties of Japanese barberry (*Berberis thunbergii*) or purple-leaf sand cherry (*Prunus cistena*), or with such perennials as pinks (*Dianthus*), lamb's-ears (*Stachys byzantina*) or meadow rues (*Thalictrum*).

### Care and propagation

*Rosa rubrifolia* is a low-maintenance plant. As a species rose, it represents a category apart from modern hybrids, which too often have been bred for large, repeat-blooming flowers at the

Illustration: Rosalind Loeb Wanke

*Rosa rubrifolia* is a rugged species rose grown for its unusual, multicolored foliage, which combines beautifully with almost all other garden plants. This specimen outside author Martin Ray's office serves as a perfect foil for June-blooming white bellflowers, a blue veronica and a soft pink primrose.

expense of vigor and form in the bush itself. This plant, however, retains its natural grace and needs no pampering. Treat it as you would most other shrubs by planting it in reasonably good, well-drained soil and giving it plenty of sun. A yearly ½-in. top-dressing of compost or manure promotes a better flower display. *R. rubrifolia* appears to suffer from no diseases or pests other than the omnivorous Japanese beetle.

Pruning consists of cutting out branches at ground level when they become too old or too weak to flower well. I haven't noticed any such fatigue in ten-year-old shrubs, however. And unlike many other species roses, *Rosa rubrifolia* doesn't sucker at the base creating thickets, so thinning, when necessary, isn't a problem.

You'll probably need to buy *Rosa rubrifolia* through a specialist mail-order firm (see Sources at right). It would be rare to find one potted in a garden center or listed in a general catalog. In your search, you may come across the hybrid 'Carmenetta', which is the result of a cross between *Rosa rubrifolia* and *R. rugosa*. 'Carmen-

## SOURCES

*The following mail-order rose nurseries carry* Rosa rubrifolia:

**Forevergreen Farm,** 70 New Gloucester Rd., North Yarmouth, ME 04021, 207-829-5830. Catalog free.

**Greenmantle Nursery,** 3010 Ettersburg Rd., Garberville, CA 95440, 707-986-7504. Send self-addressed stamped envelope for rose list.

**Heirloom Old Garden Roses,** 24062 Riverside Dr. N.E., St. Paul, OR 97137, 503-538-1576. Catalog free.

**High Country Rosarium,** 1717 Downing St., Denver, CO 80218, 303-832-4026. Catalog $1.00.

**Hortico, Inc.,** RR 1, 723 Robson Rd., Waterdown, ON, Canada L0R 2H1, 416-689-6984. Catalog $2.00 (U.S. funds).

**Pickering Nurseries, Inc.,** 670 Kingston Rd., Pickering, ON, Canada L1V 1A6. Catalog $3.00 (U.S. funds).

**Roses of Yesterday & Today,** 802 Brown's Valley Rd., Watsonville, CA 95076-0398, 408-724-3537. Catalog $3.00.

etta' is more robust and bears slightly larger flowers than *R. rubrifolia*, and is somewhat less refined as a result. It is similar enough to the true species, however, to cause uncertainties in identification, even for experts, unless the two are side by side. If you want to be precise in this matter, talk to your nurseryman before placing your order.

Once you have established *Rosa rubrifolia* in the garden, you'll be able to increase your stock by looking for seedlings at its base. They are easy to move when young. Line them out in a corner of your garden, and the following spring move the young plants to their destinations. They should flower by their third year.

One such foundling graces the entry to my office. In early spring, a mixture of small bulbs emerges below this now-mature rose and flowers before the rose leafs out. From bulbs to hips, this combination of plants allows me to enjoy a full 12 months of interest in this prominent spot. □

*Martin Ray is a landscape gardener in Gloucester, Massachusetts.*

# Hardy Magnolias

## Brilliant blossoms for colder climes

by Melvin L. Schmidt

**A** long time ago, whenever I heard the word "magnolia," I would think of Rhett Butler and Scarlet O'Hara idling away the hours beneath evergreen leaves and sweetly scented blossoms. But that scene doesn't come to mind much anymore. That's because the magnolias I've come to love are the deciduous, hardy varieties that thrive in the Northern states and bloom in early spring, before their leaves have budded out. Seeing their delicate flowers appear when winter still has the land in its grasp gives the beholder a renewed grip on life. But the best thing about these hardy magnolias is that they require very little work to keep them in full splendor.

The variety of hardy magnolias is increasing rapidly. Only a few years ago, the old standby saucer magnolia, or tulip magnolia, (Magnolia × soulangiana) was the principal hardy magnolia grown outside the South. Now, thanks to hybridization, hardy magnolias are available in white, yellow and various shades of red, ranging from pink to burgundy.

To suit your particular landscape, you can choose from shrub, spire or standard tree form. Most Asiatic magnolias bloom before the leaves emerge, while most deciduous native American magnolias bloom after the leaves have budded out. If you live in a northern state and plant an extremely early-blooming variety, like one of the star magnolias (M. stellata), you risk losing the blossoms to a late cold snap. Even so, the flowers of these early bloomers can withstand quite a bit of cold. As the result of continuous hybridizing, one or more hardy magnolias can be grown successfully in any part of the U.S.

**Blooming time and blossoms**—The star magnolias open rapidly, going from bud to full-flower within about three days in

Most species of hardy magnolias, like the star magnolia shown here, burst into bloom in early spring before the leaves appear. The blossoms of star magnolias start out as fuzzy, catkin-like buds, which adorn the tree throughout the winter months. Most varieties of deciduous magnolias are hardy to -12° F.

early spring. Large, white, daisy-shaped flowers, 4 in. to 5 in. in diameter, emerge from plump, fuzzy, gray buds on leafless limbs before almost anything else blooms. Blossom color ranges from solid white to pale pink. In the absence of the usual background of green leaves, the overall appearance is of a cloud of white butterflies taking flight on a sudden puff of chilly wind.

Other magnolias flower at different times, from relatively early in the springtime to midsummer, depending on the location in which they're being grown. The hardy varieties have blossoms of white, pink, deep wine red and a clear yellow. Blossoms can be as large as 12 in. in diameter. Some, like the star magnolias, have flat blossoms which resemble daisies, while others, such as the Kosar hybrid 'Susan', have a fan of slightly twisted petals which never fully opens into a totally flat blossom. Others, like M. × soulangiana, have cup- or tulip-shaped blossoms.

Photos, facing page and at right: Allen Rokach; above, Al Bussewitz

Some are fragrant with the scent of cinnamon, anise or lemon. Some, like 'Susan', will produce a few blossoms periodically throughout the entire summer and early fall, in addition to their regular period of bloom in spring. The catalogs describe the blossoms, so you can choose something that suits your fancy.

**Varieties**—Hardy magnolias fall into two groups: the species magnolias and the hybrid magnolias. Over the years, the original species have been improved by nurserymen who have selected superior plants and then produced identical plants from them by vegetative means such as grafting and rooting cuttings. Hybrid magnolias are created by cross-pollinating two different species and planting the resulting seeds. Superior plants from these seeds are then reproduced vegetatively to yield identical plants. Most of these species magnolias, and selections from them, are hardy to at least -12° F.

## Magnolia *(Magnolia)*

- Deciduous, shrubby tree to large tree, growing 8 ft. to 50 ft. high.

- Hardy in Zones 5-9

- Blooms early to late spring, with some varieties blooming a second time in summer. Blossoms range in color from white and yellow to pink and deep red, and range in size from 4 in. to 12 in.

- Grows in partial shade or full sun, and in moist, acidic soil.

- Prune plants when young, and only new growth thereafter.

- Wide selection of species and hybrids available, varying in size, habit, blossom color and hardiness.

The bigleaf magnolia (above) can grow to a height of 50 ft. Its large leaves show off equally large, creamy white blossoms which bloom in the summer and sometimes reach 15 in. in diameter. The umbrella magnolia (below) is nicely suited to smaller gardens because it grows from 10 ft. to 35 ft. high. Hardy as far north as Boston, this tree has attractive foliage and lovely white blossoms.

**Species magnolias for large gardens**—A hardy species magnolia suited only for larger gardens is *M. heptapeta* (formerly *M. denudata*), the Yulan or lily magnolia, which grows to 50 ft. tall. Introduced from central China about 1789, it's a tree-shaped magnolia with an ample supply of cup-shaped, ivory-colored blossoms. A selected variety with a bit of purple at the base of the blossoms is available.

If you really have a lot of space, you might want to consider the bigleaf magnolia, *M. macrophylla*. It ranges in height from 25 ft. to 50 ft. and has leaves from 6 in. to 12 in. wide and up to nearly a yard long. Its fragrant, creamy white flowers open in the summer months and expand to nearly 15 in. in diameter.

**Species for smaller gardens**—The Oyama magnolia (*M. sieboldii*), native to Japan and Korea, is a shrubby or small, tree-shaped magnolia; it grows from 15 ft. to 30 ft. tall. In addition to its small, ¾-in. white flowers with red stamens, *M. sieboldii* provides an additional bonus—yellow seed pods, which turn bright pink toward the end of August. Blooming from very late spring through most of the summer, *M. sieboldii* is one of the very few Asiatic magnolias that flower when the leaves have already emerged.

The tree-shaped umbrella magnolia (*M. tripetela*) has large, creamy white blossoms up to 10 in. in diameter, which have a musky, perhaps unpleasant, scent. The leaves are 12 in. to 24 in. long and are arranged like the ribs of an open umbrella on the tips of smooth, green branches. The seed cones turn pink in August and are very decorative. The umbrella magnolia is a small tree—from 10 ft. to 35 ft. tall—and can be grown at least as far north as Boston.

*M. quinquepeta* (formerly known as *M. liliflora*) is a shrubby magnolia suitable for a very small garden because of its height of only about 10 ft. *M. quinquepeta* should be hardy to about -12° F, and its deep purplish flowers will satisfy those who are tired of white blossoms.

If your landscape plan calls for a pyramid-shaped tree, try the anise magnolia, *M. salicifolia*, which was introduced from Japan in 1892. In contrast to the large, rich green foliage of most magnolias, *M. salicifolia* has narrow leaves like a weeping willow. The star-like, white blossoms appear in spring. Some of the selected varieties have anise-scented foliage for those who fancy licorice. This magnolia can be used in a small garden because its narrow spire grows upward to a maximum of about 20 ft., rather than spreading out sideways. It would fit nicely in a garden corner. *M. salicifolia* should be hardy to at least -12° F.

The Wilson magnolia (*M. wilsonii*) came over from China around 1908. It

Photos this page: Al Bussewitz; illustration, Rosalind L. Wanke ends up as either a shrub or a small tree depending on how you prune it when it's young. *M. wilsonii* puts forth small, 4-in. white blossoms with bright red stamens from late spring to early summer when you don't have to fret about late frosts. You can put *M. wilsonii* in partial shade. It seems less hardy than the other hardy magnolias, so you might want to consider planting this one in a microclimate.

The star magnolia (*M. stellata*), a native of Japan, is one of the true gems of the magnolia family. In addition to white and pink star magnolias, I have the Kosar hybrid 'Susan', 'Wada's Memory', and M. 'Elizabeth' in my yard. But my favorite has always been the white star magnolia. These will grow in partial shade, which is an advantage. Two of mine are thriving with only a scant half day's sun.

These are the beauties whose trembling blossoms appear against a framework of bare branches in very early spring. They are of shrubby growth to about 10 ft. tall by 10 ft. wide and sport luxuriant, dense green foliage with an inviting satiny texture that emerges after the flowers fade. An added bonus are the fuzzy, gray buds which adorn the branches all winter after the leaves fall. They look something like the unopened catkins on pussy willows. Star magnolias will grow just about anywhere in the U.S. In response to their popularity, hybridizers have worked on this species, so specialist nurseries offer a good selection.

My *M. stellata* 'Royal Star' has survived -30° F. here. If you live in an especially severe climate where you've been unable to grow a star magnolia successfully, try the similar, hardier species *M. kobus*, from Japan, which blooms slightly later and has large blossoms.

**Evergreen magnolias**—The thick, shiny, leathery-leaved evergreen magnolias don't really belong to the category of hardy magnolias, but I want to mention them because isolated specimens are found where least expected. They bloom during most of the summer, and several of the Southern magnolias (*M. grandiflora*), with their large, creamy white, lemon-scented blossoms, survive in southeastern Kansas. I have seen a picture of a specimen several stories tall on Lafayette Avenue in Brooklyn, N.Y. Another evergreen is the much-smaller-flowered, but hardier, sweet bay magnolia (*M. virginiana*). Selected hardier varieties of both these evergreen magnolias are available, so don't be hesitant about trying one in a microclimate in your yard, even in climates where the temperature dips below -12° F. They won't grow to be 60 ft. tall, but the sight of a miniature 15-ft. specimen covered with evergreen leaves when there's a foot of snow on the ground is a true delight.

*M. quinquepeta* (formerly known as *M. liliflora*) blooms in late spring and again in the summer. It's a bushy shrub, grows to a maximum height of 8 ft. to 10 ft., and is hardy to about -12° F.

The Southern magnolia, with its large, white, lemon-scented blossoms, is an evergreen and can be grown as far north as southern Kansas.

**Hybrid magnolias**—The most famous of the hybrid magnolias is the formidable *M. × soulangiana*, which some call the tulip or saucer magnolia. Everyone is familiar with the white and pink tulip- or cup-shaped blossoms which appear in early April. *M. × soulangiana* is normally grown as a globe-shaped tree which will eventually reach a height of 25 or 30 ft. Where I live, it has proved itself reliably hardy to -30° F. For large-flowering, hardy magnolias, the *M. × soulangiana* hybrids are hard to beat. There are a great many varieties to choose from in the mail-order catalogs. Take your pick. If you don't have room for one in your yard, see if your neighbors will let you plant one in their yard. I have planted quite a few trees in my neighbors' yards over the years, and nobody has complained yet.

An especially welcome addition to the magnolia hybrids is M. 'Elizabeth', which was developed by the Brooklyn Botanical Garden a few years ago. It is similar to *M. × soulangiana*—just as hardy, and begins producing its electric yellow blossoms when very young. Mine bloomed the spring following initial planting when it was still less than 2 ft. tall. This tree isn't cheap, but it's well worth its price. It is the first magnolia with true, primrose-yellow blossoms. It grows rapidly; mine grew 3 ft. last year.

*M. × loebneri*, a cross between *M. kobus* and *M. stellata*, is hardy at least as far north as Illinois and probably quite a bit farther. The blossoms are similar to those of *M. stellata*, one of its parents. Different varieties give you a choice of blossoms ranging in color from white to light pink. Some are fragrant. Quite a few varieties are available by mail order.

The Kosar and De Vos hybrids were created at the National Arboretum in Washington, D.C., during the 1950s. They comprise a very desirable group of shrubby magnolias which will form a conical, well-shaped bush up to about 10 ft. in height. The deep wine-red blossoms of the Kosar hybrid 'Susan' were described above. Mine has grown well and rapidly with only about half a day of morning sun. The blossom colors range from pink to purple and wine red, some are a combination of two of these colors. *M.* 'Ann' has cinnamon-scented blossoms. The Kosar and De Vos hybrids are hardy to at least -12° F, but don't be shy about planting them in localities where the temperature goes well below that temperature. These beauties are "toughies," but if yours doesn't survive, you're not out any more money than you'd spend on a good Sunday meal for your family.

There are so many other hybrid magnolias that you should read about them in a catalog from one of the magnolia specialists. There are magnolias for virtually every garden. All you have to do is read the catalogs until you find something that strikes your fancy and seems to stand a reasonable chance of surviving where you live.

**Hardiness and microclimates**—If you live in one of the harsher climate zones, look around your yard for a microclimate that could be a successful site for several of the hardier varieties such as *M. stellata* 'Royal Star', *M.* 'Marjory Gossler', *M.* 'Wada's Picture', or the Kosar hybrid 'Susan'. When you're searching for a microclimate, look for areas that are sheltered from the wind and where plants manage to survive several hard frosts in the fall and don't succumb until well after the other plants have gone dormant. The south side of a house, for example, is normally a microclimate where some plants can be grown that wouldn't survive out in an open yard. But even if you can't find a suitable microclimate in your yard, one of the hardier varieties of magnolia could do just fine. You'll be surprised at just how tough some of these trees can be.

The best way to determine whether or not a particular magnolia will be hardy in your area is to check the hardiness rating in the catalog and figure the plant will be hardy to five to ten degrees colder. If you can find a suitable microclimate in your yard, figure another five degrees colder. There's no absolutely certain way to do this because many factors, such as winter winds, humidity and soil conditions go into determining a particular tree's hardiness in a given location. Read the catalogs and use your good sense. You can also check with your state agricultural colleges. Don't hesitate to be a bit adventurous—the reward is worth the risk.

**Planting and transplanting**—Do not buy a bare root magnolia. Local nurserymen normally have some that were grown in their containers. Reputable mail-order nurseries will send your magnolia with the entire rootball it had in the container it was grown in. Ask that your magnolia be shipped so it will arrive shortly after you normally have your last killing freeze. As soon as you get your magnolia, water it and then plant it carefully to the same depth it was planted in its nursery container. Be very careful with the fleshy, brittle roots so you don't break off any.

Before you plant the magnolia, dig a hole about 3 ft. in diameter and 3 ft. deep. Why do you need such a big hole for such a small plant? Because all that loose soil will promote active, rapid root growth. So grow the roots, so grows the tree, as the saying goes. Secondly, you want to mix a lot of peat moss in with the soil to make it acidic, friable and well drained—all conditions your magnolia will like. If your soil is alkaline, you can acidify it by adding ammonium nitrate according to the directions on the box.

My magnolias are growing well in what we call sugar clay. This is yellow clay which is very hard when dry but reasonably friable when damp. By no means is it a high-class soil. If you start your magnolia off right in a big hole filled with reasonably good soil and peat moss, the chances are it will thrive even

## SOURCES

*The species star magnolias with plain white blossoms are quite common and are available at most nurseries and garden centers.*

*Almost all mail-order nurseries have the standard M. × soulangiana and white star magnolia, and sometimes even a couple of others, but it is better to purchase container-grown plants locally, unless you know that the mail-order nursery ships plants with a good root ball or is a nursery specializing in magnolias.*

*To acquire the more sophisticated varieties, such as 'Royal Star', you have to order from one of the following mail-order sources:*

**Gossler Farms Nursery,** 1200 Weaver Rd., Springfield, OR 97478-9663 (magnolia specialists, large selection). Catalog $1.00)

**Louisiana Nursery,** Rt. 7, Box 43, Opelousas, LA 70570 (magnolia specialists - very large selection of over 350 varieties). Catalog $3.50.

**Greer Gardens,** 1280 Goodpasture Is. Rd., Eugene, OR 97401. Catalog $1.

**Wayside Gardens,** Hodges, South Carolina 29695-0001 (small but carefully-chosen selection). Catalog is free.

*To join the Magnolia Society, write to Phelan Bright, 907 S. Chestnut St., Hammons, LA 70403 for a membership application.*

when the roots have grown out into the poor soil surrounding the hole. If your plant is in a location where it will get blown about by the wind, you need to stake it. Magnolia expert Roger Gossler of Gossler Farms Nursery advises that you should not tie the trunk of your new magnolia tightly to the stake or the tree won't develop a strong, heavy trunk. Do not plant magnolias where they will have to put up with severe winds.

If you anticipate having to transplant your magnolia after a year or two, then plant it to begin with in a good-sized plastic or fiber pot that has several holes in it. Later, when you want to transplant it, dig up the pot and carefully cut it off the root ball. This procedure will minimize damage to the fragile roots. It's not a good idea to transplant a magnolia that's been growing for more than a couple of years in its present location unless the tree is still pretty small. Transplant only in early spring and dig up as big a ball of soil as possible to minimize damage.

**Culture**—Water your magnolia thoroughly after planting or transplanting and keep the soil moist forever afterwards, but not to the point where the plant is sitting in a swamp. Fertilize in spring and midsummer with an acid fertilizer such as Mir-Acid, and follow the directions on the container. Do not fertilize after the first of August or you will promote new growth which may not harden in time for winter; the new growth will be lost to frost damage, and you won't have gained anything.

Since magnolia roots grow fairly close to the surface, do not hoe weeds under these plants. Instead, mulch magnolias heavily with straw and pull any weeds which manage to grow through the straw. The mulch will also help keep the roots cool, which is something magnolias really appreciate.

**Pruning**—Prune when your magnolia is quite young so you're cutting only small branches. Always use tree-wound paint, or at least a black or brown, oil-base enamel paint, to seal the cut. If you prune large branches when the magnolia is older, you run the risk of losing the tree from infection because a large cut may not heal, and bacteria can then enter the tree through the wound. If you must prune an older magnolia, prune the new, small branches only. To be prudent, decide on the shape of your magnolia when it is still very young, and do most of the pruning necessary to achieve this shape at that time. Always do your pruning during the summer months. ☐

*Melvin L. Schmidt practices law and grows magnolias in Wathena, Kansas.*

The hybrid tulip magnolia, or saucer magnolia, has many cultivars, with blossoms ranging from yellow-white to lavender to purple-pink and deep red. Hardy in Zones 6-9, these fast-growing hybrids have a bushy shape with an eventual height of about 25 ft.

The cultivar 'Leonard Messel', with its purplish blossoms, can be a fast-growing shrub or a small tree. It's hardy in Zones 5-9.

The cultivar 'Elizabeth' can grow 3 ft. per year or more. It's the only magnolia with true primrose-yellow blossoms.

Photos, top and right: Michael Dirr; left, Al Bussewitz

# Outstanding Crabapples
## How to make the right choice for your landscape

by Thomas L. Green

It's not hard to see why I fell for the four-season beauty of crabapples. In the spring, these small-to-medium-sized trees put on spectacular flower shows. The newly emerging leaves disappear in clouds of fragrant white, pink or red blossoms, arresting the eye and nose of the passing viewer. As the

growing season progresses, the fruits take on color and become attractive in their own right. Red, orange or yellow in color, they dangle in profusion from the branches like so many large berries. In some varieties, the fruits persist into winter, brightening a dreary season. Some crabapples also have foliage that turns a beautiful gold in the fall. And when their leaves have dropped, their interesting branching patterns take center stage. I love the sight of newly fallen snow caught on the bare branches of a crabapple.

Crabapples are adaptable trees. Given full sun, they grow well in a wide range of soils. They are also very hardy. Some cultivars can survive winter lows of -40°F (USDA Zone 2). Most crabapples also perform well in warmer climates, though few thrive in the coastal Southeast or the Southwest.

Crabapple trees come in all sorts of shapes and sizes. In form, they can be weeping, round, oval, upright or horizontal. In size, they range from 6-ft. tall shrubs to medium-sized trees, reaching 40 ft. in height and spread.

of the century. A few, such as *M. baccata*, *M. sargentii* and *M. floribunda*, remain popular as pure species, but the vast majority of the hundreds of crabapples available in the nursery trade today are hybrids of these and other species.

My introduction to crabapples came late in life. As a plant pathologist, I knew more about crabapple diseases than I did about the trees themselves. Then one day, ten years ago, one of the country's leading experts on crabapples visited me at

## Crabapples *(Malus* spp.)
MAL-us

- Shrubs to medium-sized trees grown primarily for their spring flowers and their fall fruit. Hundreds of varieties available.

- Hardiness varies according to cultivar. Some hardy to USDA Zone 2. Most will perform well in all but the coastal Southeast and the Southwest.

- White, pink or red flowers appear in profusion in April.

- Red, orange, green, purple or yellow fruit matures in early fall. Size ranges from 2 in. to less than ½ in. in diameter. Smaller fruit attractive to birds.

- Need full sun. Tolerant of a wide range of soil types, but thrive in a slightly acid, well-drained soil.

recently, nurserymen selected crabapple varieties solely for their floral display. Fruit mess and disease susceptibility weren't considered, resulting in the promotion and wide-scale distribution of crabapples that had nice flowers but some rather bad habits.

Fortunately, many crabapple cultivars not only flower beautifully in spring but also resist diseases and hold on to their leaves and fruits. With care, you can choose a good cultivar. Don't buy any old crabapple on impulse; there is still no shortage of poor performers in the trade. Instead, consider your needs and then do a little research. Consult your gardening friends, contact your cooperative extension agent, visit the crabapple collection in a nearby botanical garden or arboretum, or write to the International Ornamental Crabapple Society (see Resources on p. 60). You will be rewarded for your efforts with a tree that can give you years of enjoyment.

### How to choose a crabapple

Because of the sheer variety of crabapples, I recommend that you put together a checklist of the attributes you want your tree to have before you go shopping. Disease resistance is important, but you should also consider the size and form of the tree, and the color, size and persistence of the fruits. The flowers, beautiful but fleeting, should be the last thing on your list.

**Disease resistance**—There are four diseases that regularly plague crabapples: apple scab, fire blight, cedar-apple rust and powdery mildew. From an aesthetic standpoint, apple scab is the most serious of these diseases. Scab is a fungus that proliferates in humid climates. It appears as brown or black, sooty spots on the leaves and as corky spots on the fruits. Afflicted leaves often drop early. In years of heavy infection, highly susceptible cultivars may defoliate in July and August, leaving a bare tree during late summer and early fall. Scab is not lethal to the plant (though it may result in a loss of vigor), but few gardeners want a tree in a prominent location to drop its leaves prematurely.

Fire blight poses the most serious threat to the health of a crabapple. This bacterial disease attacks branch and trunk tissues, causing dieback. The affected blossoms, twigs and branches turn brown and wither as if scorched. If the bacteria spread to

A file of crabapples in full bloom runs the gamut of color—deep red, white, and pale and deep pink. The best crabapples offer striking spring bloom, healthy leaves and colorful fruit crops that brighten fall and winter.

Some are dense; others are loose and open. The foliage varies from coarse (similar to the texture of apple leaves) to almost fine.

Both crabapples and apples belong to the genus *Malus* in the rose family. The distinction between the two is fruit size: trees which bear fruits larger than 2 in. in diameter are classified as apples, while those bearing smaller fruits are classified as crabapples. Most ornamental crabapple species are native to Asia. Collectors introduced them to this country around the turn

the Morton Arboretum outside Chicago and opened my eyes to the beauty of our collection. Today, as executive director of the International Ornamental Crabapple Society, I spend a great deal of my time sharing my enthusiasm for these wonderful, small trees.

### Beware the bad apples

Unfortunately, many people think of crabapples as trees that lose their leaves by the end of summer due to disease and drop large, messy fruits on lawns and driveways. Until

From spring blossoms to winter fruit on bare branches, crabapples can be striking additions to the landscape. Pink buds and white flowers together on the same tree make a disease-resistant cultivar like 'White Angel' (inset) particularly appealing.

the trunk, they may eventually kill the entire tree.

Cedar-apple rust is a fungal disease that afflicts native crabapple species or hybrids with a native parent. The symptoms are yellowish or orange spots on the leaves. If the infection is severe, the leaves may drop prematurely. Cedar-apple rust is an unusual disease in that it requires the presence of native junipers to complete its life cycle. Don't plant susceptible crabapple varieties unless you know that there aren't any junipers within a mile of your yard.

Powdery mildew attacks the leaves, blossoms and fruits. It's easy to spot as a powdery white fungus covering the surface of the leaves or the fruits. Powdery mildew occurs most often in periods of warm temperatures and high humidity. It is most often a problem in the southeastern U.S.

While crabapples as a group are prone to these diseases, there are many specific varieties that show great resistance. Other varieties are disease tolerant—they are susceptible to disease, but they don't suffer the worst of the symptoms. For example, some varieties get scab but don't defoliate prematurely. Only close inspection will reveal that the disease is present.

Disease-susceptible varieties to avoid (like the plague) include: 'Hopa', 'Radiant', 'Almey', 'Aldenhamensis,' 'Eleyi', 'Kelsey', 'Oekonomierat Echtermeyer', 'Red Silver' and 'Vanguard'. Many nurseries are still offering crabapples that have serious disease problems, though some of the leading wholesale crabapple nurseries are dropping or have dropped these from production.

Because a cultivar's susceptibility to disease may vary from region to region, I, along with two colleagues, instituted the National Crabapple Evaluation Program in 1983. We selected 46 varieties that had demonstrated disease resistance in earlier evaluations and 25 test sites at universities and botanical gardens around the country. To make sure that the disease organisms were present at the test sites, we added three varieties to the list that were highly disease susceptible. Our evaluations should help provide information about which varieties perform best in different parts of the country. The table on p. 60 includes a few of the varieties that have thus far shown resistance to disease in more than one region of the country.

A cloud of flowers and buds on the disease-resistant cultivar 'Indian Summer' almost obscures the new spring foliage and branches.

The beautiful blushing yellow fruits of 'Ormiston Roy' prove that crabapples come in a range of colors to brighten the fall and winter garden.

Pictured above at approximately life size, the ½-in. fruits of 'Adams' produce a colorful display that can last well past frost.

**Size and form**—When selecting a crabapple for a landscape, it's important to consider size and form. Plant larger, rounded trees alone as specimens or mass them for dramatic effect. Medium-sized oval varieties make good patio trees. Weepers add a nice touch to an informal landscape. The multi-stemmed, shrubby crabapples have a place in a conventional shrub bed or in a large flower border; they can also be planted as a hedge. No matter how you use a crabapple in the landscape, remember to plan for the mature size of the tree.

**Fruit color and persistence**—Next consider the color of the fruits. The colors range from shades of red, orange and yellow, to green and purple. When selecting fruit color, keep in mind the background against which the fruits will appear. Yellow fruits stand out better against red or brown backgrounds; red and orange fruits look best against white or light.

The size of the fruits is also an important consideration. Crabapple fruits that are larger than ½ in. in diameter can create a mess when they drop. As the fallen fruits soften, they become slippery on paved surfaces. They also make walking or playing on the lawn unpleasant, and they may attract yellow jackets, as well. I recommend you seek out varieties with fruits smaller than ½ in. Even if they drop in autumn,

Photos: facing page, background, Staff; inset, Susan Kahn; this page, top, Edward Hasselkus; center and bottom, Staff

## A sampler of disease-resistant crabapples
*Fruit size of all listed varieties is ⅝ in. or smaller.

| Variety | Flower color | Fruit color* | Mature Height/Width (in ft.) | Comments |
|---|---|---|---|---|
| 'Adams' | Red | Red | 20/20 | Round form. One of the best reds. |
| 'David' | White | Red | 15/15 | Round form. |
| 'Donald Wyman' | White | Red | 25/25 | Round form. Good post-frost color. |
| 'Indian Summer' | Red | Red | 20/20 | Spreading vase shape. Good fruit display. |
| *Malus floribunda* | Pink and white | Amber | 20/30 | Hardy to Zone 4. Good fruit for fall birds. |
| 'Molten Lava' | White | Red | 15/15 | Horizontal form. Fruit attractive to birds. |
| 'Prairie Fire' | Red | Red | 20/20 | Spreading vase shape. |
| 'Professor Sprenger' | White | Orange | 25/25 | Round form. |
| 'Red Jewel' | White | Red | 15/15 | Oval form. Good post-frost fruit color. |
| 'Sugar Tyme' | White | Red | 20/20 | Round form. Good post-frost fruit color. |
| 'White Angel' | White | Red | 20/20 | Spreading vase shape. Good post-frost fruit color. |
| 'Zumi Calocarpa' | White | Red | 20/30 | Horizontal form. Birds attracted to fruit in spring. Flower buds are red. |

they won't make a mess. Most desirable of all are varieties, such as 'Zumi Calocarpa', that bear fruits which remain on the branches until spring or until birds eat them. These persistent fruits usually shrivel and drop unobtrusively by spring.

Fruits that are ½ in. in diameter or smaller are bite-size for birds. The fruits of some crabapples soften in the fall and can be very attractive to migrating birds. On other varieties, the fruits soften after frost and provide a valuable source of food for birds that don't migrate for the winter or for spring migrators. Gardeners interested in attracting birds to their gardens should become familiar with these wonderful fall and winter crabapples. I receive great enjoyment watching robins, starlings and waxwings work over my Japanese flowering crab (*M. floribunda*) each autumn.

**Flowers**—To get an idea of the range of available whites, pinks, reds and shades in between, visit a botanical garden or a university test plot at flowering time. Note that the color and shape of the bud as it expands can add a great deal to the beauty of the flower show. On some varieties, such as *M. floribunda* and 'Zumi Calocarpa', red buds give way to pink or even white flowers. Flower colors may also change as the flowers age. Red and pink flowers often fade to lighter hues

## RESOURCES

For more information on crabapple varieties that are suited to your area, consult your local cooperative extension agent, or write to the **International Ornamental Crabapple Society**, c/o Dr. Thomas L. Green, Morton Arboretum, Lisle, IL 60532.

There are several large, wholesale nurseries which carry a wide selection of crabapples. If your local nurseryman doesn't carry the variety of your choice, ask him to special order a tree direct from a wholesaler. The Crabapple Society may also be able to help you locate a particular variety.

and finally to white before they go by. The presence of buds and flowers at various stages of maturity together on the same tree is stunning.

Some trees have a tendency to flower every other year, a phenomenon known as alternate bearing. Since the principal reasons for growing crabapples are the flowers and the resulting fruits, I recommend that you look for annual-bearing varieties. Sargent crabapples (*M. sargentii*) and the cultivar 'Mary Potter' are alternate bearing. Both are shrubs, and since there are few other varieties with comparable form and ornamental characteristics, they are still widely grown and recommended.

## Crabapple care

Crabapples require no special maintenance. Water once every three to four weeks during dry periods. Apply fertilizer if a soil test indicates that you should. Don't over fertilize, especially with nitrogen, which stimulates vegetative growth at the expense of flower and fruit production. Like most other fruit trees, crabapples are prey to pests. Japanese beetles, borers, mites and tent caterpillars are the most common visitors. None of these pests is reason enough to avoid planting crabapples.

Crabapples benefit from occasional pruning. Prune after flowering every three or four years to maintain the desired form and to remove overlapping, rubbing, and interfering branches. Also prune out the watersprouts—branches that ascend vertically from the trunk and branches.

Crabapples may produce shoots, called suckers, from their roots. Grafted trees are especially prone to suckering. Propagators at many wholesale nurseries increase their stock by grafting one variety (the scion) onto the roots of another. If the growth rates of scion and rootstock are not the same, (especially if the top is slower), the roots may send up suckers. On some varieties, suckers are a major problem. If left unpruned, they can become a separate tree that bears no resemblance to the tree you planted. When you shop for a crabapple, look for trees that started life as rooted cuttings. In general, they produce fewer suckers than grafted trees. If you purchase a grafted tree, look for one with a "non-suckering" rootstock, such as M-111 or M-106. These rootstocks don't eliminate suckering, but they do reduce it. If you buy a tree that suckers, prune the suckers off every year after the spring growth spurt.

## The perfect crabapple

The perfect crabapple would be resistant to diseases. It would bear small, beautiful, persistent fruits that attract birds. It would be free of watersprouts and suckers and have just the right size and shape. And, of course, it would have an abundant display of fragrant flowers. While the perfect crabapple has yet to be found, many varieties come close enough. □

*Thomas L. Green is a plant pathologist at the Morton Arboretum in Lisle, Illinois, and executive director of the International Ornamental Crabapple Society.*

# Redbuds

## Clouds of spring color from small ornamental trees

by J.C. Raulston

**R**edbuds are among the most striking sights of early spring. These small, spreading trees flower before the leaves appear, clothing their bare twigs and branches with reddish buds that open in a profusion of small, pea-like, magenta-pink flowers. During the rest of the year, redbuds have other attractions: the heart-shaped leaves hang in graceful tiers and turn a clear yellow in fall; and older trees often develop a picturesque open framework of large branches.

Redbuds make handsome specimen plants. To my eye, they look especially good against a background of dark-green conifers. The contrast accents the constantly-changing color of the flowers, which varies as they open and age and as the light shifts during the day (one reason the flower color is hard to photograph accurately).

While all redbuds have a family resemblance, the genus Cercis offers a wide range of heights, shapes, flower colors and foliage. There are seven to nine species of Cercis worldwide, and a number of named selections—trees of uncommon appeal found in the wild and propagated by nurseries. They range from 3-ft. shrubs to 50-ft.-tall trees, with flowers of pure white, pink, magenta or deep purplish-red. The species and selections produce simple flowers, with one exception, the double-flowered selection 'Flame' (also called 'Plena'), which grows much faster than the species and bears fewer seed pods because many of the stamens develop as petals. Foliage variations include the deep purple leaves of the selection 'Forest Pansy', and the stunning white-variegated leaves of 'Silver Cloud'. Both are most showy in spring with new growth. Their distinctive colors are most dramatic in cooler regions, and tend to fade in warmer climates.

There is a redbud selection or species adapted to the climate of nearly every

Clothed in pink flowers, an Eastern redbud blooms in profusion. Flowering in early spring before their leaves appear, redbuds are among the most striking heralds of the new growing season.

Photo: J.C. Raulston

region of the U.S. The native Eastern redbud, Cercis canadensis, has a vast range, covering much of the eastern U.S. and Plains states, and parts of Mexico. The Western redbud, C. occidentalis, grows wild from Arizona to Oregon. There are five to seven foreign species found wild from Spain to the deserts of Israel, and throughout China. The hardiest redbuds—C. canadensis selections from the northern limit of their U.S. range—survive winter lows in Zone 4. The most heat-tolerant redbuds will grow in Florida, Texas and California.

## Starting with seeds or a tree

Redbuds are not as widely known or grown as they should be, mainly because named selections are hard to find. Redbuds do not come true from seeds. Grafting is the typical method for propagating named selections, but redbuds are difficult to graft. They also have a reputation for being hard to transplant when dug from the nursery field. Nonetheless, a few mail-order nurseries offer named selections, and your local nursery may be able to order rarer selections from a wholesaler (see Sources on p. 65). At the North Carolina State University Arboretum in Raleigh, North Carolina, we have the world's largest collection of redbuds. We encourage gardeners and the nursery trade to try new selections and species, and are always glad to hear about promising trees and nurseries offering rare redbuds.

If you like adventure, you can grow redbuds from seeds, though you will be limited to the species. You can collect seeds from local trees or buy seeds from a dealer. Harvest the dried seed pods any time from October through spring (an early harvest may avoid insect damage to the seeds). Break the pods and remove the smooth brown seeds. The hard seed coat must be broken (scarified) for water uptake—the simplest method is to file, scrape or nick the coat. Put the scarified seeds in a plastic bag with damp peat moss or vermiculite, and store them in the refrigerator at 38° F to 40° F for three months before sowing in spring. You can also sow seeds outside in fall and let winter scarify and chill them.

Seedling redbuds grow rapidly and transplant well. Many gardeners, impatient for a large tree, buy a ten-footer at the nursery and are disappointed when the tree suffers in transplanting and makes poor growth or dies. Seedlings are an alternative. You can buy and transplant a one-year-old seedling in spring and expect 4 ft. to 7 ft. of growth the first year. If you start trees from seeds, they can reach 10 ft. in two or three years when properly watered and fertilized.

## Eastern redbud

The eastern redbud, at 25 ft. to 40 ft., is the largest, fastest growing and most tree-like of all redbuds. It has 3-in.- to 6-in.-diameter light green leaves with pointed tips. A white-flowered selection called 'Alba' is offered by several mail-order nurseries. There are many variations in the plant across its vast native range, which extends from New Jersey to Nebraska in the north, and central Florida to below Mexico City in the south. The Texas and Mexico populations are almost certainly geographical variants—ecotypes—of the Eastern redbud, but they are often named as separate species. For convenience, I'll call the Texas redbud C. reniformis and the Mexican redbud C. mexicana, and I'll describe them separately.

The eastern redbud is widely adapted. It does well in a variety of soils, though it prefers deep loams with good drainage and moisture, and it tolerates drought better than flooding. I recommend liming acid soils to produce a pH between 6.0 and 6.5. The plant grows well in partial shade, but full sun encourages the best shape and the most prolific flowering.

Trees from different parts of the native range tend to vary in hardiness. The northernmost redbuds I know are in lower Zone 4, beautiful specimens at the Minnesota Landscape Arboretum. Summer climate influences hardiness. In England and the Pacific Northwest where summers are too cool to mature and ripen the wood, the Eastern redbud is much less hardy than in its native range. In those climates, it's injured by winter temperatures that would not begin to bother it in areas with baking summer heat.

Recently, concern has arisen in the Northeast regarding canker, a fungal disease of branches and trunk which is causing increasingly-widespread loss of redbuds in the landscape. I believe the problem mainly affects plants in three categories: old, declining trees; environmentally-stressed trees; and trees grown in conditions too different from

## Redbud (*Cercis* spp.)

- Small tree that clothes itself in pink or white flowers in early spring before the leaves appear.

- Spreading branches and attractive, usually flat leaves in tiers.

- Seven to nine species, including several natives. The hardiest will grow in Zone 5.

- Slightly acid soil, about pH 6.5, but the native Western redbud tolerates alkaline soil.

- Grows and flowers best in full sun, but tolerates partial shade.

A streetside tree in summer shows the typical spreading shape and tiered foliage of the Eastern redbud, with a native range from the heat of Texas to the cold of Zone 5.

Photo: Michael A. Dirr

those in their native range. The reme-
dies for stress are good siting and good
care. The remedy for ill-adapted
plants is buying wisely. If you live in
a northern area, avoid trees from
a southern nursery, unless you can
determine that the trees were grown
from seeds collected in a northern state.
If you live in Zone 4 or 5, you can
buy dependably hardy seeds of the
Eastern redbud, collected in upper
New York state, from Sheffield's Tree
& Shrub Seed Co. in New York. Likewise, gardeners in the deep South
should avoid seeds from northern
sources. There's no remedy for old age—
redbuds evolved as relatively short-
lived pioneer plants of woodland
margins, with a normal life span of 20
to 30 years in the wild. When a tree
declines, it's usually best to remove it
and replace it with a young redbud.
You may, however, cut a declining
tree to the ground in spring after flowering, let the stump produce sprouts,
and then thin the new growth to make
a multi-trunked clump.

### Texas redbud

Texas redbud (C. reniformis) is a superb
ornamental, with two outstanding selections. The tree is small, usually 15 ft.
to 20 ft. tall. The thick, leathery leaves
are 2 in. to 4 in. wide (smaller than
those of the Eastern redbud), with
rounded tips and a glossy, dark green
upper surface. Native in Texas,
Oklahoma and Mexico, the Texas
redbud is nonetheless hardy in Zone 6
(-10° F), provided it gets sufficient
summer heat.

I consider 'Oklahoma', a Texas
redbud selection, to be one of the finest
flowering trees in existence. It has highly glossy, very leathery leaves that are
extremely attractive all summer, and
dark reddish-purple flowers that are
the "reddest" of redbud blossoms.
Discovered as a wild seedling in
Oklahoma's Arbuckle Mountains in
1964, this selection so surpasses the
Eastern redbud in beauty that most
gardeners would grow nothing else—
provided they could find it. Unfortunately, 'Oklahoma' is difficult to propagate, so plants are scarce and expensive. It's listed by some nurseries
as Cercis 5 'Oklahoma'. One caution:
should you chance on a nursery selling
quantities of cheap 'Oklahoma' plants,
first look for glossy leaves, and then
check how the plants were propagated. I once encountered an honest but
misguided grower selling so-called
'Oklahoma' trees that were actually
seedlings grown from seeds collected in
Oklahoma. Like any redbud selection,
a true 'Oklahoma' can be propagated
only by grafting.

As these fallen leaves show, the redbud's autumn color ranges from pale green to clear yellow.

Unusual foliage graces two redbud selections.
At left are the unique, variegated leaves of
'Silver Cloud', and at right are the also unique,
deep purple leaves of 'Forest Pansy'.

Photos: at top, Pamela Harper; below, Michael A. Dirr

In full flower, a Chinese redbud shows the multiple trunks spreading habit and dense bloom that are characteristic of the species.

The other selection of Texas redbud is 'Texas White', which has the same superb foliage as 'Oklahoma', but pure white flowers. It is stunning in bloom. On the West Coast a white selection of the Eastern redbud, 'Alba' is often mistakenly sold as 'Texas White'. A true 'Texas White' has thick, leathery, glossy foliage.

## Mexican redbud

The leaves of Mexican redbud (C. mexicana) not only have a glossy surface, like Texas redbud, but also an undulating margin that makes them the most beautiful of all redbud leaves. Apparently the glossy leaves appear with age. The foliage of young trees resembles the matte foliage of the Eastern redbud. Mexican redbud leaves vary from 1 in. to 6 in. in diameter on seedlings from different regions.

The growth habit of the Mexican redbud varies greatly, from densely twiggy, 5-ft. shrubs to 15-ft. trees, but in general, the plant is finer-textured

Stiff, glossy leaves distinguish the Texas redbud which is hardy in Zone 6. The author considers 'Oklahoma', a Texas redbud with deep pink flowers, to be the most ornamental redbud selection available.

than most redbuds. Small Mexican redbuds would make excellent specimens for city homes and townhouses, and even can be grown in tubs. Hardiness depends on the source and on summer heat, but plants can survive in Zone 6 (-10° F).

## Western redbud

Though Western redbud (C. occidentalis) usually grows as a dense, multistemmed shrub, 3 ft. to 7 ft. tall, it can reach 18 ft. tall, with a tree form. Considered hardy in Zone 7, the plant has blue-green leaves with rounded or notched tips. The foliage turns yellow-red in fall.

Western redbud is best adapted to soils with pH above 6.5 and a climate with dry, hot summers and cool, wet winters. Like most woody plants of the West Coast, it does not thrive in the East, even where it is nominally hardy. The East's acid, poorly drained soils and drenching summer rains usually induce root decline. (I believe Eastern

Photos: top, Pamela Harper; below, J.C. Raulston

gardeners could grow the Western redbud if it were grafted onto the roots of the Eastern redbud.)

Though Western redbuds vary greatly in the wild, no selections have been named and offered for sale. But Western gardeners should watch for the introduction of a white-flowered selection which was found wild in the Sierras. The Saratoga Horticultural Foundation Inc., San Martin, California, and the Rancho Santa Ana Botanic Garden, Claremont, California, are working to introduce it.

### Chinese redbud

The Chinese redbud (C. chinensis) is a highly ornamental species that deserves greater use. It is native over a wide range in China, and can be grown here in Zones 6 to 8. Although the Chinese redbud grows to 50 ft. in the wild, in cultivation it is almost always a multi-trunked shrub or tree, 8 ft. to 14 ft. tall. The plant usually grows rigidly upright, with glossier, darker green leaves than those of Eastern redbud. The flower buds are much more densely arranged on the stems and provide a more solid color display. Chinese redbud also tends to flower slightly earlier than our native species.

There is an outstanding selection of Chinese redbud called 'Avondale' which will likely become widely grown in the U.S. It was found as a seedling in the Avondale suburb of Auckland, New Zealand. The flowers are not only darker than usual but are borne in such profusion that they completely hide twigs, branches, and even large limbs. Redbuds can produce flowers directly from older branches and even from the trunk, a rarity among non-tropical trees, but 'Avondale' surpasses all the selections I know for its profusion of flowers on old wood. The Arboretum's tree flowers on the main 3-in. diameter trunk as low as 1 in. from the ground!

After flowering, 'Avondale' sets so many seed pods that it has little energy for growth. Removing the young pods a few weeks after bloom promotes much greater growth and ensures better flowering the following year.

'Avondale' grows well in the East, and is also performing well in the Pacific Northwest, where it will probably prove hardier than most Eastern redbuds.

There are two other selections of Chinese redbud, both growing in the U.S. but unavailable from nurseries, as far as I know. One is 'Alba', a white-flowered form. The other is a dwarf selection, 'Nana', which matures at 3 ft. to 5 ft. in height and spreads slowly to form clumps. I doubted that 'Nana' was in the U.S. until I recently found a whole field of old plants at Aldridge Nursery, a Texas wholesaler.

### SOURCES

*Few nurseries offer more than one or two redbuds. The sources listed here offer a considerable number of redbud species and selections, or redbud seeds.*

**Greer Gardens,** 1280 Goodpasture Island Rd., Eugene, OR 97401. Catalog, $3. An extensive list of redbud species and selections.

**ForestFarm,** 990 Tetherfiner Rd., Williams, OR 97544. Catalog, $3. An extensive list of redbud species and selections.

**Arrowhead Nurseries,** Dept. F, 38 Watia Rd., Bryson City, NC 28713-9683. An extensive list of redbud selections, including 'Silver Cloud'; some available in spring, others in fall. List free.

**Aldridge Nursery, Inc.,** P.O. Box 1299, Von Ormy, TX 78073. Offers Texas and Mexican redbuds, including several selections. Wholesale only, but will ship small orders UPS if ordered by a local nursery. Trees shipped bare root mid-January to mid-February only, so northern gardeners will have to hold trees in containers for spring planting.

**Yucca Do Nursery,** P.O. Box 655, Waller, TX 77484. Catalog, $2. Texas and Mexican redbud seedlings.

**J.L. Hudson Seedsman,** P.O. Box 1058, Redwood City, CA 94064. Catalog, $1. Seeds of Western and Mediterranean redbud.

A young Chinese redbud covers its branches and trunk with bloom. This is the selection 'Avondale', noted for exuberant flowering.

Unfortunately, though, the plants are too large to ship.

### Mediterranean redbud

The Mediterranean redbud (C. siliquastrum), native around the Mediterranean Sea from Spain to Israel, is superbly adapted to alkaline soils and dry-summer Mediterranean climates. Rarely grown in the U.S., it would seem well adapted for the Southwest and West. Surprisingly, it is the only redbud species that grows really well in England's cool, moist climate, and it also thrives here in North Carolina. Gardeners in the Pacific Northwest and the East in Zones 6 to 9 should try it.

In Europe, old plants of the Mediterranean redbud reach 40 ft. in height, but plants in cultivation are more commonly seen at 15 ft. to 20 ft. The flowers are the typical redbud magenta, and the rounded leaves are 3 in. to 5 in. in diameter, with heart-shaped bases. Ten selections have been made in Europe, but none are available in the U.S. Gardeners who want to grow the species can buy seeds.

### Rarities and fantasies

Of the remaining redbuds, all of them rarities which have never been sold in the U.S., the ultimate connoisseur's plant is the chain-flowered redbud (C. racemosa). All horticultural writers proclaim it the most beautiful of redbuds, with pendulous 2-in. to 4-in. chains of 20 to 40 pink flowers. I'm excited that a few nurseries will begin to offer trees in two years or so. Unfortunately, the chain-flowered redbud is reported as hardy only in Zone 8 (10°F), or maybe Zone 7 (0°F). I know of flowering trees in Seattle and Washington, D.C. I think plants will likely do best in mild areas of the Pacific Northwest and the Gulf-Atlantic coastal areas.

I like to think that redbuds are a world waiting to be discovered. I hope an enterprising hobbyist will collect the many species and cultivars and cross them, combining their best traits to create irresistible new hybrids. Can I dream of a dwarf, twiggy shrub with glossy, purple, wavy-edged leaves and pure-white flowers in chains—and hardy in Zone 4? ☐

---

J.C. Raulston directs the North Carolina State University Arboretum in Raleigh, North Carolina, which includes the largest collection of redbuds in the world. Friends of the Arboretum receive Raulston's informative newsletter. For a year's membership, send $25 to NCSU Arboretum, Dept. of Horticultural Science, Box 7609, NCSU, Raleigh, NC 27695-7609.

# Fringe Trees
## Small beauties yield a cloud of bloom

The frothy, white blooms of a native fringe tree, also called old-man's-beard, make it an unusual addition to the spring landscape.

by Rob Nicholson

I am awed each year by the beauty of fringe trees. They are so floriferous that for two weeks in spring they look more like clouds than plants. Widely adapted and small enough for any property, they deserve wider use.

Fringe trees belong to the genus *Chionanthus* (from the Greek *chion*, snow, and *anthus*, flower) in the olive family. Taxonomists battle over the exact number of species. Three are accepted by almost everybody—two American natives and one from the Far East. All thrive with minimal care in average, slightly acid soil in a sunny or partly shaded location. Pests and diseases are rarely a problem.

### The American fringe trees

The better known of the American fringe trees is *C. virginicus*, commonly called old-man's-beard. The fragrant flowers are held on panicles, or clusters, 4 in. to 8 in. long. The 1-in. long petals, usually numbering four to a flower, are pure white in color and strap-like in shape. Individually, the flowers are only mildly interesting, but because they appear in profusion on each panicle, and the panicles in turn blanket the tree, the effect is astounding. As one backs away from a tree in flower, the airy white panicles coalesce, and the plant reads as a solid white mass. Flowering begins before the new leaves are fully extended, so the plant initially appears as a fleecy mass of white, punctuated by a few spots of fresh green. The leaves continue to develop during the bloom period, creating a more dappled effect.

Old-man's-beard takes the form of a small, single-stemmed tree or a large, multi-stemmed shrub, and it

usually grows broader than it is tall. The largest specimen I've seen is 25 ft. tall and 30 ft. wide. The leathery, oval, 3-in. to 8-in. long leaves are a shiny, dark green above and a pale, dull green below.

The tree grows wild along the banks of streams and ponds from southern Pennsylvania to central Florida and as far west as eastern Texas, but it is far hardier than its native range might suggest. I know of a specimen growing in Norwich, Vermont—USDA Hardiness Zone 4 (-30°F).

The only drawback of old-man's-beard is tardiness. At the Arnold Arboretum in Boston, Massachusetts, old-man's-beard is almost always naked when the lilacs are in full bloom in mid-May. But as lilac-blooming season winds down, they come alive and are in full flower for about two weeks in early June. The late appearance of the foliage makes old-man's-beards look awkward when featured. Try using them as lawn trees or along the edges of a property. They might also work well as a hedge.

The other North American species of *Chionanthus* is the pygmy fringe tree (*C. pygmaea*), which is native to central Florida. The pygmy fringe tree rarely grows taller than 8 ft. and puts on a beautiful spring flower show. The pygmy fringe tree is listed as endangered, so collecting specimens without a permit is illegal. The plant is hard to find in nurseries, but holds the promise of becoming a choice plant for shrub borders.

## The Chinese fringe tree

As beautiful as the American species are, I prefer the Chinese fringe tree (*C. retusus*). Like the American fringe trees, the Chinese species cloaks itself with a cloud of shimmering white flowers in late spring, but its smaller, shinier leaves and its shorter flower panicles give the plant a finer texture. I also find its naked architecture more appealing than that of many-stemmed, gangly American specimens. A full-grown specimen can be a superb focal point in a medium-to-small sized garden, offering some ornamental interest in almost every season. The Chinese fringe tree leafs out earlier than the native fringe tree does, but begins flowering about a week later. The Chinese fringe tree appears hardy only into Zone 6 (-10°F)

The fruits of a Chinese fringe tree dangle from the branches like clusters of tiny plums.

A blizzard of 1-in. long, strap-like petals in long panicles cloaks a descending branch of a Chinese fringe tree.

## Fruits

After flowering, some fringe trees set fruit. The trees can be male, female, or mostly one or the other, but only trees bearing female flowers can set fruit. Because most nursery plants are grown from seeds, there is no way of knowing what the sexual persuasion of your plant is going to be. To improve your odds of seeing the ½-in., dark blue, plum-like fruits, plant more than one tree. The neighborhood birds, which devour the fruits as they mature in late summer or fall, will thank you.

*Rob Nicholson is greenhouse manager at Smith College in Northampton, Massachusetts.*

### SOURCES

*A number of mail-order nurseries carry both* Chionanthus virginicus *and* C. retusus. *Here are three from different regions of the U.S.*

**Forestfarm,** 990 Tetherow Rd., Williams, OR 97544, 503-846-6963. Catalog $3.

**Wayside Gardens,** 1 Garden Lane, Hodges, SC 29695-0001, 800-845-1124. Catalog free.

**Yucca Do Nursery,** P.O. Box 655, Waller, TX 77484, 409-826-6363. Shipping season is October through March. Catalog $3.

the photo above) measures 21 ft. tall and 33 ft. wide, with a circumference of 144 ft. at the dripline. To push through the branches and walk beneath this green giant is like entering a Druid's cathedral or a Scottish burial cairn.

These large specimens leave me in awe, but my garden is much too small to accommodate one. As an alternative, I'm training different cultivars of weeping hemlock up a stretch of wooden fence — 'Green Mound', 'Pendula', and a cultivar of the Carolina hemlock (*Tsuga carolin-*

*iana*), 'La Bar's Weeping'. As each grows, I'll choose a strong branch to act as a leader and tie it onto the fence, just as I would stake up a tomato. In time, I hope to have a vertical tapestry of hemlock foliage.

Although hemlocks can be found on rocky slopes in the wild, these populations may have evolved to grow in those conditions. Cultivated weeping hemlocks prefer evenly moist, acid soil, with full sun or partial shade. They're extremely hardy, tolerating USDA Zone 4 (to -30°F) conditions.

Weeping hemlocks are sometimes

staked at the nursery. If you're satisfied with their height, there's no need to continue staking them. If you'd rather have a taller section of straight trunk, stake up last year's growth until it reaches the desired height, then remove the stake. As each tie is added farther up the stem, remove the one below it.

## Weeping katsura— a temple treasure

Another weeping deciduous tree only recently brought to these shores has

Though the weeping parrotia is not yet commercially available, it's a promising landscape tree, as shown by this specimen at Kew Gardens in England (above). In the fall, its leaves turn raucous colors, and in the winter, its mottled bark is revealed. The weeping katsura (below) is a fast-growing, problem-free tree that forms an airy canopy. In the autumn, the heart-shaped leaves turn a soft orangy-red to apricot-yellow color, emitting an elusive, honey-scented fragrance.

been a horticultural treasure in Japan for decades. *Cercidiphyllum,* the katsura tree, is a genus with two species from Japan and one variety from China. Both Japanese species have a weeping form: *C. magnificum* 'Pendulum' and *C. japonicum* 'Pendulum'.

The beautiful foliage of weeping katsura is its most distinctive attribute (see photo, bottom right), since the flowers are inconspicuous and its platy gray bark only subtly interesting. When they first unfold, the rounded heart-shaped leaves

Photos: top, Michael Dirr; bottom, Staff

# WHY TREES WEEP

Rob Nicholson's article brought to mind the wide range of weeping trees I've seen—some with branches barely arching above the ground, others that drooped like an upside-down mop, and still others with branches held stiffly like ribs of an open umbrella. What, I wondered, makes them weep?

After many conversations with Nicholson and several tree researchers around the country, I discovered that much more is known about how weeping trees grow than why they weep. The lowest-growing weepers, Nicholson explained, such as Coles prostrate hemlock (*Tsuga canadensis* 'Coles'), are unable to form a leader, which is the dominant, highest extension of the main stem on a standard upright tree. Instead, their main stem and branches grow horizontally, close to the ground. A medium-height weeper, like Sargent's weeping hemlock, initially sends the main stem upward in a leaderlike fashion, but only a few degrees above horizontal. The following year, new branches arch over the stem, and year after year, the arching boughs slowly stack up.

Taller weepers generally have a distinctly upright leader with mostly pendulous lateral branches. The weeping katsura is an interesting example. New branches that form in the spring are all pendulous. Each autumn, one of the topmost pendulous branches draws itself upright, while the other branches remain weeping. The next spring, the process begins anew. In this way, the tree gains some height while maintaining an overall weeping form.

To find out *why* trees weep, I turned to Dr. Sally Taylor, a professor of botany at Connecticut College. Like the other researchers I spoke with, she said that scientists have only just begun to scratch the surface of this complex topic.

As background, Dr. Taylor told me that a branch on any tree grows from a bud at the angle at which the bud is inserted on the tree. Each tree species has a specific angle of bud insertion that is genetically determined: if the angle is very small, the branches grow upward; if the angle is very large, like that of weeping trees, the branches grow outward or even downward.

The branch growth of upright and weeping trees also differs. A branch of an upright tree normally reacts to gravity by growing upward. As the branch bends down under the weight of leaves and side branches, a specialized kind of wood known as reaction wood forms, forcing the branch to right itself.

In some species of weeping trees, mutations cause different responses to gravity and bending. The shoot tips of weeping willows, for example, react to gravity by drooping. Other weeping trees have a normal response to gravity that would orient the shoot tip upward, but older shoots or branches have too little reaction wood to keep them from sagging. As the walls of cells in these branches mature, they lignify and thicken, cementing the downward bend in place permanently. Lateral branches may begin growing outward from the weeping branch, but without reaction wood, they too eventually droop down.

Mutations such as these occur periodically in all woody plants, and some recent genetic studies have begun to pinpoint the exact nature of the mutation in weeping trees. For instance, scientists have shown that the weeping habit of peaches is controlled by a single recessive gene. Studies like these certainly increase our understanding of the phenomenon, and may even pave the way for the creation of new species of weeping trees in the future. □

---

*Nancy Beaubaire is an associate editor at Fine Gardening.*

*These nurseries sell one or more of the weeping trees discussed by the author:*
Carroll Gardens, P.O. Box 310, Westminster, MD 21157. 800-638-6334. Catalog $2.00.

Coenosium Gardens, 6642 S. Lone Elder Rd., Aurora, OR 97002. Catalog $3.00.

Forestfarm, 990 Tetherow Rd., Williams, OR 97544. Catalog $2.00.

Foxborough Nursery, 3611 Miller Rd., Street, MD 21154. 301-836-7023. Catalog $1.00.

Gossler Farms Nursery, 1200 Weaver Rd., Springfield, OR 97478. 503-746-3922. Catalog $1.00.

Greer Gardens, 1280 Goodpasture Island Rd., Eugene, OR 97401. 503-686-8266. Catalog $3.00.

Twombly Nursery, 163 Barn Hill Rd., Monroe, CT 06468. 203-261-2133. Catalog $2.00.

are a soft rosy-khaki color. From a distance the branches appear to be strung with copper coins. When fully developed, the leaves are an enchanting soft parrot green held upon pinkish-red petioles like overlapping shingles, somewhat reminiscent of an aristolochia vine. The leaves have a tantalizing honey-scented fragrance in the fall. Autumn leaf color ranges from soft orangy-red to apricot-yellow. My weeping-katsura leaves turn buttery-yellow each fall, but I've seen color variation from year to year on others.

The weeping katsura has proved to be one of the most vigorous and fastest-growing of all pendulous trees at the Arboretum. Dr. Hayao Iwagaki, who sent us the original scions from Japan in 1981, also sent us photos of a 150-year-old specimen at Ryugengi Temple that measures 50 ft. tall and about 25 ft. wide, with a trunk circumference of 10 ft. Nearly 20 ft. up, the trunk splits into three main stems, the tree's overall habit resembling that of a tall, thin weeping willow or

beech. One of the original grafted weeping katsuras planted in the Boston area has grown 20 ft. tall and 12 ft. wide, with a stem caliper of 4 in.

In the landscape, weeping katsuras look good planted as specimens or in groves. They're particularly attractive massed on a lawn or planted along a walkway to form an allée. I've lined a short walkway on my property with weeping katsuras grafted onto 6-ft. standards. As the trees grow, I'll prune off the leader so they won't grow taller than 8 ft. to 9 ft. I'll also prop out the branches between the plants with bamboo poles so the trees will eventually create a flowing wall of green hearts.

The weeping katsura is a clean, problem-free tree. I assume that it's hardy to USDA Zone 5 because I've seen the normal species growing near the icebox city of Sapporo, Japan, withstanding winter lows of -20°F. Grown in a constantly moist soil in full sun, weeping katsuras thrive once they're established. They take a year or two to settle in after transplanting, however, so don't let them dry out during that time.

Many nurseries graft weeping katsuras at ground level, but you can stake the trees to whatever height you want, allowing the arching branches to form above that point. These trees don't require pruning, but they can be shaped when they're dormant.

## Weeping parrotia— a Persian weeper

My fourth selection, weeping parrotia (*Parrotia pendula* 'Persica'), isn't yet commercially available, but I hope that mentioning this exceptional tree will encourage nurseries to propagate it. There are no mature weeping parrotias in the United States, as this native of Iran has only recently been introduced here. The original specimen was selected from a batch of seedlings in 1934 by the propagator at England's Kew Gardens, Charles Coates, though several clones probably exist today. The tree is rare, however, even in England, where it grows to a compact mound with arching pendulous branches. In our climate, its flowers are inconspicuous, but interesting on close inspection, producing a mass of cherry-red stamens bound in a chocolate-colored sheath.

Weeping parrotia is most appealing in the fall and winter. Its autumn colors are a riotous mix of pink, maroon, yellow and orange, and the tan, silvery-gray and white mottled bark contrasts nicely with the winter snows. The few weeping parrotias we're growing at the Arboretum are thriving in a moist, loamy soil, in full sun as well as in partial shade. So far, weeping parrotia has been disease- and pest-free, and promises to be a glorious addition to our gardens.

This weeping beech (*Fagus sylvatica* 'Tortuosa') is particularly dramatic during the winter when its twisted branches are outlined with a dusting of snow.

## Weeping beech—
## Quasimodo in wood

To my eyes, the premier pendulous beech is the parasol or monster beech, *Fagus sylvatica* 'Tortuosa'. Rather than hanging in a graceful cascade like those of the weeping cherry, the beech branches grow outward in a haphazard zigzag and then writhe their way earthward, sometimes intersecting and fusing together like a contortionist in wood. The weeping beech is truly a tree of mythical appearance: one expects it to be the backdrop for Alice's raucous tea party or to find baby dragons nested within its boughs.

Nearly a century ago, collectors recognized the ornamental value of the weeping beech, a rare natural mutation found in beech forests in northern Europe. Since then, several weeping-beech cultivars have been developed, all grafted onto the standard European beech (*Fagus sylvatica*), among them 'Pendula', 'Purpureo-pendula' and var. *miltonensis*.

During the summer, the trees look like mounds of minty-green leaves from a distance, but upon closer inspection you can see the gnarled trunk, festooned with carbuncles, or knobby growths, and the twisted branches growing like snakes in a frenzy. In the autumn, the yellow and tan leaves are attractive, but perhaps weeping beeches are at their best during the winter when their radical architecture is highlighted by a fresh snow.

The best specimens I've seen of 'Tortuosa' are two 100-year-old trees here at the Arnold Arboretum (one is shown above). To my mind, they're the most stunning trees in our collection of thousands. Planted in a grove of huge beeches from around the world, each is 20 ft. high with a spread of 40 ft. Don't let their size intimidate you. Weeping beeches grow slowly. Often sold as 1-ft.-tall, bareroot trees, they won't grow much more than 6 ft. to 8 ft. tall and equally as wide in ten years, though you should allow enough room in the landscape for their eventual size.

Weeping beeches grow best in a deep, moist loam, reflecting their woodland origin. Interestingly enough, they grow more vigorously in full sun, though they can tolerate partial shade. Hardy to USDA Zone 5, they survive winter lows of -20°F. Because they grow so slowly, there's no need to prune them except for nipping off suckers arising from the rootstock. I haven't observed any insect or disease problems.

Unless you want a gothic feel as you come up the driveway, I think weeping beeches look best in a backyard, at the corners of a property, or planted on a steep slope above a patio, where their novel structure can be shown off to good advantage. They would also be an attractive focal point on college campuses, alongside pedestrian plazas and in large courtyards. □

*Rob Nicholson is on the propagation staff at the Arnold Arboretum in Jamaica Plain, Massachusetts. He gardens nearby.*

A heavy crop of berries glows among the oval leaves of 'Burfordii', a cultivar of the Chinese holly.

Hollies are varied and distinctive landscape plants, as this photo shows. Their lustrous foliage persists year-round, and female plants bear colorful fruits. The low mound in the foreground is 'Rotunda', a cultivar of the Chinese holly. The tree with red fruits is 'Nellie R. Stevens', a widely-planted, hybrid holly.

Drooping, lance-shaped leaves and 3/8-in.-long elliptical berries characterize the Kashi holly.

Photos: top and bottom right, Fred Galle; bottom left, Pamela Harper

# Hollies

## Deck the garden with these versatile, evergreen shrubs and trees

by Fred C. Galle

ollies deserve more use. With their dense foliage of shiny, evergreen leaves, they offer a striking alternative to more familiar broadleaf evergreens such as rhododendrons. Among the hundreds of holly cultivars, there are plants adapted to all but the harshest growing conditions, as well as plants for every garden setting. The dwarf cultivars, most of them low-mounded or spreading plants under 3 ft. tall, are suited to rock gardens and for planting in front of taller shrubs. The many medium-sized hollies are useful in foundation plantings and hedges, and the taller hollies make attractive screens, hedges and wind breaks, as well as specimen trees. Hollies are also valuable as companion and background plants for many other shrubs. If that's not enough, in late fall and winter, the lustrous foliage is complemented by crops of berries in colors that include red, orange, yellow, black and light, yellowish white. Deck the halls with holly, but enjoy them in the garden, too.

### Where hollies grow

As a group, hollies are widely adapted. Worldwide, from the temperate zone to the tropics, there are over 780 evergreen species and 30 deciduous species (numbers that make holly enthusiasts and breeders dream). Among evergreen hollies, the U.S. nursery trade offers more than 30 species and hundreds of cultivars. One cultivar or another thrives in most of the eastern U.S., from east Texas to Minnesota and Florida to southern Maine, and throughout the Pacific states from southern California to northern Washington. For example, the English holly, *I. aquifolium*, grows beautifully in the coastal zones of the Pacific Northwest, where it enjoys the maritime

---

### Holly *(Ilex* spp.)

- Evergreen shrubs and trees with distinctive, shiny, dense foliage; wide range of species and cultivars, from dwarfs to 60-ft.-tall trees; growing range includes most of eastern U.S., and the Pacific States.

- Three hardy deciduous species that brighten winter with crops of berries; growing range covers much of the U.S.

- Most evergreen species hardy to Zone 7 or Zone 6, with a few hardy to Zone 5; some deciduous hollies are hardy to Zone 3.

- Need full sun and well-drained soil.

- Young plants need regular watering for several years, until they become established.

- Hollies have many landscape uses—as specimens, in hedges, in foundation plantings, in mixed borders with other shrubs, as backgrounds and screens, and as container plants.

---

humidity, but in the South and Southeast, it is chancy. There, the plants need a bit of shade and prompt watering to provide relief from the heat and occasional droughts of summer. But the American holly, *I. opaca*, thrives in the South and Southeast. Native from Florida to New England, it tolerates heat and cold. And there are hybrid hollies—crosses between two or more species—adapted to a wide range of conditions.

In general, evergreen hollies are not suited to conditions in most of the Plains States and the Southwest, though plants in protected locations may grow fairly well. Wind and sun are the chief winter dangers—like all broadleaf evergreens, hollies can dry out when the ground is frozen. (In most regions that are inhospitable to evergreen hollies, gardeners can grow deciduous hollies, which drop their leaves in fall and brighten the winter with their berries. See "Deciduous Hollies" on p. 78.)

### Choosing hollies

The main limits on growing hollies are cold and heat. Most evergreen hollies are hardy only to Zone 6 (-10°F) and a few are hardy only to Zone 7 (0°F). If you live in Zone 5, where the average minimum winter temperature is -20°F, you can choose from among three species: the American holly (*I. opaca*), the hybrid blue hollies (*I. × meserveae*), and the inkberry (*I. glabra*), a black-fruited, multi-stemmed shrub. In the heat and humidity of warmer zones, some hollies suffer. The English holly, for example, grows best in Zone 7. Farther south, it struggles. (See the table on p. 77 for the northern and southern limits of commonly grown hollies.)

There are three ways to check if a holly is suited to your climate. The first is the catalogs of mail-order holly nurseries. They generally explain the hardiness and tolerance for heat of their listings. The second is to ask at a good local nursery that carries hollies. You won't find a wide range of hollies, but the ones for sale are usually adapted to your region. (There are exceptions, I'm afraid. Here in the Atlanta area, for example, local nurseries offer the attractive, small, spiny-leaved Okinawan holly, *I. dimorphophylla*. Atlanta is in Zone 8, but the Okinawan holly is hardy only to Zone 9.) Finally, you can learn a lot about hollies for your area from the American Holly Society and its nearby members (for more about the Society, see Resources on p. 78).

I can't really say I have favorite hollies—I enjoy all plants, and my favorite is the one I'm looking at—but I'll suggest some species and cultivars you might consider before you pick a holly for your garden. The lusterleaf holly (*I. latifolia*) is a big plant, with large, spiny leaves, best suited as a specimen in a sizable garden. The clusters of fragrant, yellow flowers draw attention to the plant in the spring. The long-stalked holly (*I. pedunculosa*) has wavy, glossy, smooth-edged leaves that set off the berries, which are borne on long stalks, an unusual characteristic among hollies (botanists call the stalks peduncles). The yaupon holly (*I. vomitoria*), a small-leaved native of the South, has many uses in the landscape. Among its cultivars, there are hollies with low compact habits ('Dwarf Yaupon'), pendulous branches ('Folsom Weeping,' available in male and female plants), yellow berries ('Wiggins' or 'Wiggins Yellow') and red berries ('Grays Greenleaf'). Yaupons are excellent in the woodland garden, or used in large masses, as tall, pruned hedges, or as

Variegated hollies are striking accent plants. Above is 'Silvary', a cultivar of the English holly. The cream-white margins of the leaves dramatize their spiny outline. Below is 'O'spring', a yellow-variegated cultivar of the Chinese holly.

Small-leaved hollies can resemble boxwoods. Here the densely-branching dwarf cultivar 'Helleri' makes a low mound along a slate path.

specimen small trees with multiple trunks.

There are a number of hybrids between holly species that seem to tolerate a wider range of growing conditions than most hollies. The so-called "blue" hollies (*I. × meserveae*), are hybrids whose dark, rough leaves have a distinctive bluish green sheen. Some are hardy in Zone 5. Their dark foliage and vivid berries contrast strikingly. The cultivar 'Nellie R. Stevens', a hybrid of the English and Chinese hollies, may be the most widely available of all hollies. It is a 15-ft. to 20-ft. tree with red berries.

Among the available holly cultivars, the leaves vary widely in size, shape and appearance. English, Chinese and American hollies and their hybrids tend to have broad leaves that are 2 in. to 3 in. long, often edged with stiff, sharp spines, while Japanese hollies, yaupons, and inkberries have far smaller leaves—most less than 1 in. long, with toothed but spine-free edges. Some hollies have striking, variegated leaves, with light-green to near-white edges. They make distinctive specimens and good background plants to make a small property seem larger. The best-known variegated hollies are cultivars of the English holly such as 'Silvary', 'Golden Milkboy', 'Golden Milkmaid', 'Ingramii', 'Silver Milkboy', 'Silver Milkmaid', 'Silver Queen', 'Wieman's Moonbrite' and

Photos: top, Fred Galle; bottom and center, Pamela Harper

others. There are two variegated American hollies, 'Steward's Cream Crown' and 'Steward's Silver Crown'. Two of the best-known variegated Japanese hollies are 'Snowflake', with a yellowish-white margin, and 'Midas Touch', with yellowish margins.

Consider berry color before you decide on a holly. Most colors show best in direct sun, set off by dark foliage around them. However, yellow berries look bright even on cloudy days. Here are a few yellow-fruited cultivars: for the Chinese holly, the cultivar 'D'Or'; for the American holly, 'Canary', 'Princeton Gold' and 'Betty Nevison', among others; for the English holly, 'Bacciflava', 'Berigold', 'Wieman's Yellow Pillar' and 'Yellow Beam'; and for the Japanese holly, 'Butterball', 'Forty-Niner', 'Honeycomb', 'Ivory Hall', 'Ivory Tower' and 'Sunshine'.

## How to get berries

Hollies are dioecious, having separate male and female plants. The flowers of male plants produce pollen. The flowers of female plants, when pollinated, produce the familiar holly berries.

If you want hollies that bear fruits, you must buy plants of both sexes that flower together. The timing is close. For example, the lusterleaf holly and the Chinese holly flower in early spring. Neither species will pollinate the American holly (I. opaca), which flowers later in the spring. Good garden centers sell compatible male and female plants, and the catalogs of mail-order holly nurseries recommend suitable pairs. As a rule of thumb, you need only one male plant for every 15 to 20 female plants, provided they flower at the same time.

## Using hollies in the landscape

One of the holly's chief attractions is its dense, shiny foliage. In general, the leaves are stiff and smooth, often with a surface sheen that looks polished. Since most hollies branch a lot, the leaves cluster together, or overlap, making a solid canopy that suits them for background and privacy plantings. Hollies with small leaves can be sheared to good effect. The plants tolerate the stress of shearing, regrow readily and produce denser foliage.

Hollies make attractive hedges. The screen or hedge can be of one species or cultivar ('Foster No. 2', an upright hybrid of the American holly, is often used in hedges), or a planting of several species and cultivars. At Callaway Gardens in Pine Mountain, Georgia, a long, unpruned hedge of 'Burfordii,' screens a highway. In another part of the garden, plants of yaupon holly and 'Burfordii' together screen a parking lot. At my own home, on a wooded property, I'm planting an informal screen of holly species, hybrids and cultivars.

Many hollies are small, compact plants suited to patio-growing or bonsai. For growing in larger pots and boxes for the porch or patio, I suggest the cultivars 'Blue Girl', 'Blue Princess' and 'Golden Girl', which are all blue hollies. Several cultivars of the Chinese holly, including 'Carissa' and 'Dwarf Burford', are often used in large containers. I'm trying a new introduction of American holly, 'William Hawkins', in a large box for the porch. A male plant, 'William Hawkins' has beautiful, very narrow, spiny leaves. It is a real conversation piece. I enjoy growing small-leaved dwarf hollies for my bonsai friends. Some Japanese holly cultivars with bonsai potential are 'Dwarf Cone', 'Dwarf Pagoda', 'Piccolo', 'Delaware

## A partial list of hollies for the garden

F = female, M = male.

### English holly, *Ilex aquifolium*

Most are upright and pyramidal. Leaves spiny, 2 in. to 3 in. long. Zone 6 to 8b.

'Angustifolia', F & M, small, narrow, spiny leaves. 'Beautyspray', F. 'Ebony Magic', F, Zone 5b, also reported as a Blue Holly. 'Escort', M. 'Gold Coast', M, variegated. 'Golden Milkmaid', F, variegated. 'Longspray', F. 'Shortspray', F, compact, upright. 'Silvary', F, variegated. 'Silver Edge', F, variegated. 'Wieman's Globe', F, compact, rounded. 'Wieman's Moonbright', M, variegated. 'Yellow Beam', F, yellow fruits.

### *Ilex* × *altaclarensis*

Crosses of I. aquifolium and I. perado, often slightly hardier than English holly. Leaves 2⅜ - 5 in. long, usually spineless or with very small spines.

'J.C. van Tol', F. 'Wieman's Favorite', F. 'Winter Queen', F. 'Wilsonii', F.

### American holly, *I. opaca*

U.S. native. Usually upright, pyramidal. Leaves usually spiny. Zones 5-9.

'Canary', F, yellow fruits. 'Croonenberg', F, old cultivar. 'Jersey Princess', F, glossy foliage. 'Lady Alice', F. 'Maryland Dwarf', F, low, spreading. 'Miss Helen', F. 'William Hawkins', M, very unusual, narrow leaves.

### Topal holly, *I.* × *attenuata*

Hybrids of I. cassine or I. myrtifolia and I. opaca. Leaves 2 in. to 4 in. long, usually spineless, or with few spines. Zones 7-9.

'Alagold', F, narrow leaves, yellow fruits. 'East Palatka', F, broad leaves. 'Foster No. 2', F, very popular; upright, pyramidal; leaves spiny. 'Foster No. 4', M, good pollinator. 'Hume No. 2', F, leaves usually spineless. 'Savannah', F, leaves nearly spineless.

### Japanese holly, *I. crenata*

Over 400 cultivars. Leaves ½ in. to 1 in. long. Black fruits. Zones 6 to 9.

(Very Dwarf) 'Dwarf Pagoda', F, compact, upright. 'Fairyland', F. 'Dew Drop', F. 'Jersey Jewel', M, similar to 'Dwarf Pagoda'. 'Delaware Diamond', M, mounding. (2 to 3 ft. high) 'Beehive', M. 'Helleri', F. 'Prides Tiny', F. (4 to 8 ft.) 'Convexi', F, convex leaves often turn yellowish in summer. 'Glory', M, upright, mounding; very hardy. 'Green Lustre', F, upright, spreading. 'Rotundifolia', M, upright, rounded. (Tall) 'Highlander', M, upright, pyramidal. (Variegated Foliage) 'Midas Touch', M, leaves blotched yellow. 'Snowflake' ('Siro fukrin'), F, irregular, whitish margin.

### Chinese holly, *I. cornuta*

Upright, mounding shrubs. Leaves quadrangular and spiny at corners to elliptical and spineless. Fruits typically red. Usually set fruit without pollination. Zones 7 to 9, occasionally 6b.

'Anicet Delcambre' ('Willowleaf'), F, spineless leaves. 'Burfordii', F, very popular, spineless leaves, 15-20 ft. high. 'Carissa', F, sparse fruiting; spineless leaves; to 4 ft. high. 'Dwarf Burford', F, dense, up to 8 to 10 ft. 'O' Spring', F, leaves variegated, fruits very sparce. 'Rotunda', F, spiny, dwarf.

### *I. cornuta* × *pernyi* hybrids

Compact, pyramidal. Leaves spiny 1 in. to 1¾ in. long; fruits red. Zones 6b to 9.

'Cetus', F, squarish leaves. 'Red robe', F. 'Red Delight', F. 'Dr. Kassab', F. 'Lydia Morris', F, broad pyramidal.

### Yaupon holly, *I. vomitoria*

Native and popular in Southeast. Fruits usually red. Zones 7-9.

'Dwarf Yaupon' ('Nana'), F, compact, rounded, to 6 ft.; sparse fruits. 'Folsom Weeping', F & M plants available; upright; pendulous branches. 'Gray's Greenleaf', F, upright, spreading; abundant fruits. 'Gray's Littleleaf', M. 'Wiggins', F, yellow fruits; upright, spreading.

### Inkberry, *I. glabra*

Often-overlooked natives. Leaves ¾ in. to 1½ in. long, spineless. Fruits usually black. Salt tolerant. Zones 5 to 9.

'Ivory Queen', F, fruits white. 'Princeton Compacta', F, compact, upright. 'Nordic', F. 'Shamrock', M.

### Lusterleaf holly, *I. latifolia*

Large trees, upright, pyramidal. Leaves oblong, 3 in. to 6 in. long. Fragrant, yellow flowers. Red fruits in clusters. Zones 7 to 9.

### Long-stalked holly, *I. pedunculosa*

Large shrubs or small trees, upright, pyramidal. Leaves spineless. Red fruits on long peduncles like small cherries. Zones 5 to 9.

### Other hybrid hollies

'Blue Girl', F, 'Blue Boy', M, 'Blue Princess', F, 'Blue Prince', M, 'Blue Angel', F, 'Blue Stallion', M, 'Golden Girl', F: yellow fruits. Large compact shrubs known as blue hollies', Zones 5-8. 'China Boy', M, and 'China Girl', F, large shrubs; leaves quadrangular, spiny; red fruits; Zones 6a to 9. 'Emily Bruner', F, large shrub to small tree, pyramidal; leaves spiny; Zones 6b to 9. 'Mary Nell', pyramidal; glossy, spiny leaves; red fruits; Zones 6b to 9. 'Nellie R. Stevens', pyramidal; leaves usually spineless; Zones 7 to 9. 'Rock Garden', F, compact plant, 12-16 in. high; Zones 6a to 9.

Hardier than evergreen hollies, deciduous hollies brighten the winter months with vividly-colored berries.

# DECIDUOUS HOLLIES

Deciduous hollies are at their best in winter. They drop their leaves in fall, and brighten the dormant months of the year with such heavy crops of bright red or yellow berries that the plants look painted. Until recently, deciduous hollies have been the Cinderella of the holly family, neglected and overlooked, but lately they are gaining notice, and good cultivars are being offered by the nursery trade.

Gardeners can buy three species and a few hybrids of deciduous holly. One species is the winterberry (*Ilex verticillata*), a small-to-medium-sized shrub, generally 6 ft. to 8 ft. tall. It is native from Nova Scotia and Wisconsin to Florida, and hardy to Zone 3. Plants are usually multi-stemmed. The medium-sized, light green leaves lack the spines of evergreen hollies, and the ¼-in. berries are generally bright red. The

berries, which look like small, green peas at first, color in late summer to early fall, while the leaves are still green, producing a very pleasant contrast of red and green. The berries persist after the leaves fall, but blacken and drop after severe freezes of 10° F or lower.

Several cultivars of winterberry are available in the nursery trade. 'Christmas Cheer' is a small plant with heavy crops of small, red berries.

---

Diamond' (also known as 'Elton') and 'Jersey Jewel'. Other dwarf hollies for bonsai include the relatively new 'Rock Garden', a hybrid introduced in 1984, and the English holly cultivar 'Angustifolia'.

## Planting and care

Hollies grow best in full sun, and tolerate a wide range of soils. They prefer soil that is light, well-drained and rich in organic matter, but will grow in heavy clay soil if there is reasonably good drainage. On clay soil, you can improve drainage several ways: bury drain tile before planting, mound up lighter soil and plant on the mound, or remove the top 6 in. to 10 in. of soil and replace it with lighter soil, sloping the excavation so water runs off to lower ground. On clay soil, and sandy soil as well, it helps to add lots of organic matter. Hollies prefer a pH of

6, but grow well at any pH between 5.5 and 7. If the soil is moderately acidic, about pH 5.5, you can grow hollies with rhododendrons and azaleas. The dark, dense holly leaves make an attractive combination with the paler, more open foliage of those shrubs.

Dig a generous hole when you plant hollies. Like all woody plants, they take time to recover from planting. A big hole encourages their roots and spares the plant from competition. Hollies are sold in containers or balled and burlapped. Whichever you buy, dig the planting hole at least two times as wide as the root system and just deep enough to keep the plant at the same level it grew in the container or nursery field. If you have a container plant with tangled and circling roots, spread them out while planting. I recommend filling the planting hole with soil enriched with some form of aged organic mat-

Photos these two pages: J. Bon Hartline

'Winter Red' is a medium-sized shrub with dark leaves and excellent crops of bright red berries. Its cut branches keep without water. 'Sunset' is a vigorous shrub with large berries. 'Cacapon' is a dwarf upright shrub with small, red fruits. Another good dwarf, probably a hybrid, is 'Red Sprite', which grows 3 ft. tall and bears large fruits.

Another native species of deciduous holly is the possum haw or swamp holly (*I. decidua*), a large shrub or small tree that usually has multiple stems, but can be trained to a single trunk. It grows wild from central Illinois and Missouri east to Virginia and south to Florida and Texas. It is hardy to Zone 5. The swamp holly needs more room in the garden than the winterberry. A vigorous plant can reach 20 ft. in height and width. It also tolerates moist to wet soil...I have seen it in river bottoms where water covered the roots for three months at a time. The berries are borne singly and in clusters of two or three, in a range of colors from bright red to orange. The berries begin to color in mid-fall, and can persist on the tree for more than a year, though most years, on my rural property, birds clean the plants by Christmas. Robins seem to eat more of the berries than do any other bird.

There are several cultivars of swamp holly. Those with medium-to-large berries include 'Warren's Red', 'Pocahantas', 'Council Fire', and 'Sundance'. There is one yellow-fruited variety named 'Byer's Gold', but it is difficult to propagate and not available except from collectors.

The Japanese winterberry (*I. serrata*) is also a deciduous holly. It's a small, slow-growing, twiggy shrub. There are a few hybrids of the Japanese winterberry and the U.S. winterberry: 'Harvest Red', 'Autumn Glow' and 'Sparkleberry', among others. They are larger plants, and bear heavy crops.

As with all hollies, the plants of deciduous hollies are either male or female. In order to get a winter display of berries, you need to grow a male plant that flowers at the same time as your female plants, no more than several hundred feet away. A holly nursery (see Sources listed on the opposite page) will suggest suitable companions.

—J. Bon Hartline, Anna, Illinois

Some cultivars of deciduous holly can bear huge crops: here is 'Council Fire', a cultivar of the native *Ilex decidua*.

ter, and leaving a raised rim to hold water. I fertilize lightly at planting, water thoroughly and mulch.

Fertilizing and watering help hollies establish themselves. I usually fertilize newly-planted hollies for several years with a 10-5-5 fertilizer. In late winter, I apply 1 lb. of fertilizer per inch of trunk diameter in a circle 3 ft. or larger around the plant. I prefer using a slow-release fertilizer. Hollies often respond well to an early summer application of fertilizer at half the winter rate. And a bit of urea or other nitrogen-rich fertilizer in late summer keeps plants with heavy crops of berries from developing yellowed foliage. Young hollies need regular watering for several years. Make sure they get a minimum of 1 in. of water a week during the growing season.

Hollies regrow well after pruning. I enjoy cutting greens for the holidays, and have no worry about stunt-ing the plants. Otherwise, aside from occasional thinning, I prune very little. Although many hollies can be sheared, I prefer plants with natural forms. If you must prune severely to keep a plant small or remove diseased branches, the best time to do it is early spring, just before new growth starts. Pinch the new growth to prompt branching and keep the tree full.

If you grow hollies that are adapted to your area, they will have few troubles with pests and diseases. I spray pesticides only for control after I see a problem rather than following a general spraying program.  □

*Fred C. Galle is former director of Callaway Gardens in Pine Mountain, Georgia, and a past trustee of* The Holly Society of America, Inc. *He gardens in Hamilton, Georgia.*

The picturesque branching pattern of deciduous oaks adds interest to the landscape in late fall and winter, as this white oak demonstrates so well. White oaks thrive in a wide range of soil conditions and climates, and have beautiful purplish fall color.

# The Mighty Oaks
## Tough trees to beautify your landscape

by Guy Sternberg

If you're looking for a tough, long-lived, widely adapted, handsome group of landscape trees, oaks fit the bill. Within this ancient and diverse genus are species that can thrive in the best, and handle many of the worst, planting sites. Some oaks are adapted to a broad range of conditions; others are tailored to grow in extremely harsh ecological niches. Most oaks are tree-size, though some grow no larger than a big shrub.

All oaks have staying power. Hundred-year-old specimens are not uncommon, enriching the landscape far beyond the lifetime of the gardener who plants them. For a modest investment, oaks offer a shady green canopy, a picturesque silhouette, and vivid fall color, if they're deciduous.

I've been fascinated with oaks for nearly 30 years, and I spend much of my spare time growing, observing and hybridizing them in my landscape and private research arboretum, Starhill Forest. I grow about 35 species here in the Midwest, and have observed many more in my travels around the country. I'd like to recommend some outstanding oaks for home landscapes in the Midwest, East and South. (If you garden beyond the ranges of any of the oaks I'll describe in this article, I'd encourage you to look at local nurseries and arboreta for oaks that are well adapted to your region.) All of the oaks I'll introduce here are mostly deciduous, so they'll survive in colder winter climates better than the more tender evergreen oaks growing in the West and Southwest. All are native to the United States, so you'll probably find at least one oak that's adapted to your growing conditions.

To get started growing oaks, try to purchase them from a local nursery, which is most likely to sell those species adapted to your locale. For less commonly available oaks and those you might want to start from seed, collect your own acorns in the fall or check the mail-order sources listed on p. 84.

American oaks are normally divided into two groups: red oaks, which are unique to the Western Hemisphere, and white oaks, which include species native to Europe and Asia as well. Different structural properties make white oak better suited for oak barrel construction and red oak for outdoor treated lumber, but for the gardener, the most important distinctions are in appearance and seed maturation. White oaks have whitish bark, rounded leaves and acorns that mature in one year, while red oaks have darker bark, bristle-tipped leaves and acorns that require two years to mature. For convenience, I've grouped the oaks I recommend by these categories, too, first describing the larger and then the smaller species within each group.

## Red oaks

All discussions of landscape oaks should begin with a brief look at the **pin oak** (*Quercus palustris*), the species that many gardeners unfortunately think is the only oak. The pin oak is a nurseryperson's dream—easy to propagate and transplant, and rapid-growing, with a very marketable "Christmas tree," juvenile branching habit. But in the landscape, pin oak most often is a problem tree. Unless it's pruned like a lollipop, the tree won't fit in the average yard without its pendant lower branches usurping the entire lawn. In boulevard plantings, the low twiggy growth also can become a traffic hazard. Pin oak is notoriously intolerant of soils with high pH, a trait that frequently isn't expressed until the tree is well established in the landscape and the guarantee has expired.

Except for those who have the moist, acid soil preferred by pin oak and plenty of ground-level room to accommodate its drooping lower limbs, this is the oak of the past. For the 1990s and beyond, there are many other truly outstanding oaks. Fortunately, as the demand for quality landscape trees increases, a wider variety of oaks is becoming available in the nursery trade.

The **northern red oak** was one of the first oaks to follow pin oak into popularity throughout much of the United States. It's one of our hardiest oaks, growing naturally throughout the Midwest and East and as far north as Lake St. John, Quebec. This handsome, pollution-resistant species has a clean, uncluttered branching pattern, brilliant crimson or ocher fall color, and attractive dark bark with smooth ridges that look almost like stripes on vigorous specimens. Northern red oak is easy to transplant, particularly when it's small. If moved when it's 2 in. or less in diameter, the tree recovers quickly, and once established, it's quite drought-resistant. (Many oak species form deep taproots, making it difficult to transplant larger trees successfully.)

A fast-growing tree, reaching 30 ft. tall in about 20 years, the northern red oak can become one of our largest deciduous trees in a relatively short time. Typically, a mature specimen reaches 75 ft. or more in height with a spread of 50 ft., depending on the soil. This species is amenable to most average soils, but responds very well to rich, well-drained, moist clay-loam. Like most oaks, it prospers in a sunny site. The acorns vary in size from tree to tree. I'm currently making selections for well-formed trees with large acorns for wildlife plantings, as well as some with

small acorns, which will minimize litter problems in the landscape.

In southern regions, especially where soils are poorly drained, **Shumard's red oak** is an almost identical substitute for the northern red oak, which it resembles in appearance, size and fall color. Another closely related, beautiful southern species useful in drier soils is the **southern red oak.** Its dark-green glossy leaves, which change to red-orange in autumn, are particularly attractive. Those who want a tree more reminiscent of the pin oak's form and foliage might try the **scarlet oak** on upland, sandy sites, or the faster-growing **nuttall oak** in heavier soils

The ability of this water oak to tolerate poorly drained, compacted soils has made it one of the most popular medium-size oaks planted in the South. Though this specimen is fairly young, it has become a prominent landscape feature.

and low ground, which is also easier to transplant. Both of these trees develop brilliantly-colored red leaves in the fall.

The **shingle oak,** cold-hardy throughout most of the central midwestern and eastern states, seems to have been created purely for landscape horticulture. Its uniform, dense growth habit is comparable to that of pin oak, with a slightly more rounded and less pendulous canopy. As a medium-size tree, it's better suited to the scale of residential suburbia than some of our larger oaks, though ultimately it may reach 50 ft. to 60 ft. tall, with an equal spread. Shingle-oak acorns are small and inoffensive from a litter standpoint, sifting down among blades of grass or chunks of mulch until they're claimed by squirrels or birds.

The shingle oak is easily transplanted, and is one of the oaks most adapted to a variety of exposures and soil types. Its fall

color is interesting, if not outstanding, varying from greenish-gold to crimson to a warm russet-brown. Many of its leaves persist through most or all of the winter, adding to this tree's ornamental and screening value.

Southern gardeners who find the shingle oak appealing might try two similar oaks better adapted to warmer climates—the **willow oak** and the popular **water oak.** Both are at home in wet or tight soils, as well as in soils with good drainage, and both have foliage and habits akin to those of the shingle oak.

For gardeners who don't even have enough room to accommodate a medium-size tree such as the shingle oak, one of the so-called scrub oaks, which maintain a compact form, might do. The **blackjack oak,** for example, is a dense small tree, usually reaching only 30 ft. tall and 30 ft. wide, about the size of a large crab apple. This pleasant-looking tree sports red to red-brown, persistent fall foliage, and grows well in the central Midwest and South. Although often slow-growing and unkempt in its more rigorous native habitats, which range from dune sand to adobe clay, the blackjack grows fairly rapidly into an attractive, tough little tree under cultivation. Since the taproot of the blackjack oak is very long, it's best to transplant it at a young age or to grow it from seed. Other scrub oaks such as the **eastern bear oak,** which is hardy north to Maine, and the **southern turkey oak,** which has a more southerly range, also can be domesticated into attractive small-yard trees, about the size of a crab apple. Both species grow in a wide range of soils, as long as the soil is well-drained. All of these scrub oaks have beautiful fall color, ranging from the russet-orange of the blackjack oak to the scarlet of the turkey oak. They are impervious to drought, and might even serve well as hedges or trained as topiary.

## White oaks

The standard bearers for the white oaks, **bur oaks,** must have been the species singled out by Andrew Jackson Downing, a prominent 19th-century nurseryman, who described "our finest and hardiest oaks—rich in foliage and grand in every part of their trunks and branches." An adaptable inhabitant of many landscapes—prairie groves, savannas, and upland and riparian forests—the bur oak grows throughout the South, Midwest and East, from south Texas northward to the latitude of Reindeer Island in Lake Winnipeg, Manitoba. This species is the archetype of permanence and venerability throughout its vast range.

Bur oak begins life as a slow-growing, awkward, irregularly branched sapling, the ugly duckling of oaks. But once it has attained a trunk diameter of 2 in. to 3 in., it begins a transformation into a rugged, massive monarch with a potential life span measurable in multiple centuries. Bur-oak leaves, while lacking the autumn brilliance that enlivens some other oaks, are dark and lustrous in summer, with bright, grayish lower surfaces that flash in the wind.

As the tree matures, the corky, ridged, dark-gray bark and picturesque branching become even more attractive. Under favorable conditions, bur oak can reach an immense size in old age, 70 ft. to 80 ft. tall with an equal spread. Ideal growing conditions also can coax the bur oak into episodic flushing, in which buds break their normal summer dormancy and add a second year's worth of growth. This tends to compensate for the species' usual slow growth rate. Bur oak is undaunted by heat, cold, drought, temporary flooding, a wide soil pH range and city conditions. Even climbing children probably won't damage it.

Bur-oak acorns, like those of northern red oak, vary considerably in size among different geographical races of the tree. But unlike the acorns of red oak, those of bur oak can taste so sweet that selections have been made for nut-tree orchard planting. The acorns do not constitute a long-term litter problem if squirrels and other wildlife or livestock have access to them. Even my dogs eat them!

Because bur oak puts down particularly deep roots, it should be transplanted when it's still a small tree, preferably with a trunk diameter, or caliper, of less than 2 in. Trees that have been undercut by the nursery several years before you purchase them will be easier to transplant. (Undercutting is a process in which the taproot of a small tree is severed below ground to encourage development of lateral roots.) Bigger specimens can be moved with a mechanical transplanter that will reach deeply into the ground. Bur

Oaks, as a group, have much to recommend them for the home landscape: longevity, toughness, adaptability to a wide range of soils and climates, and rich leaf color. The spectacular color of this scarlet oak, a tree well suited to growing in southern gardens with sandy soil, adds a striking look to the fall landscape.

oak also does well grown from seed, or tended as a spontaneous volunteer from an existing tree.

For wetter soil conditions and ease of transplanting, try some of the bur oak's first cousins, such as the **overcup oak,** the **swamp white oak** and the **swamp chestnut oak.** All are large trees with attractive bark, nice foliage and sweet acorns. The overcup oak is a round-headed, lustrous-leaved, southern swamp look-alike of bur oak. Native from the lower Ohio Valley southward, it can be grown at least as far north as central Illinois, if the trees are grown from northern seed sources. The more-northerly swamp white oak, which grows up in southern Ontario, is probably the easiest white oak to transplant. It's slightly smaller than the overcup oak, with interesting-looking peeling bark on its branches, like a birch. Like the overcup oak, it thrives in tight or soggy soil, but neither tree shares bur oak's toler-

ance of high pH soils. Swamp chestnut oak has about the same northerly limits as overcup oak, but grows into a taller, limbless, majestic specimen with fiery red fall color, a marked contrast to its very white bark. When planted on high ground, the swamp chestnut oak seems more sensitive to drought than the overcup or swamp white oak.

For a drought-tolerant chestnut oak, try the **rock chestnut oak,** one of the more readily available oaks at landscape nurseries. And if extremely high soil pH is your concern as well, choose the **yellow chestnut oak,** an oak distinguished by its golden fall color. Both thrive throughout the Midwest, East and South.

Then, of course, the familiar **white oak** is always a favorite. The massive, dramatic framework of an ancient white oak, with its spreading branches, is a Druid's dream. Although possibly less cold-hardy and picturesque than bur oak, the white

oak has a more easterly range. This species has excellent purplish fall color, but is horticulturally limited by its slow growth, shade intolerance, and difficulty of transplanting, even when young. It's also less tolerant of alkaline or wet soils. White oak may not be the one you choose to plant, but like bur oak, this is a tree you thank your great-grandparents for planting. Perhaps we all should consider leaving such a legacy for our great-grandchildren.

As with the red oaks, there are some white oaks that are scaled to smaller spaces. The **post oak,** suited to cultivation in the East, Midwest and throughout the South, is usually a medium-size tree, eventually reaching 40 ft. tall, though it can grow larger over time. Its leathery, glossy, dark foliage yields a fairly good russety color over an extended fall season. Once established, the post oak is drought-immune, but it is extremely slow-growing and must be transplanted when small. A

## Landscape oaks at a glance

| Common name (Botanical name) | USDA Zone | Aver. mature height (ft.) | Comments |
|---|---|---|---|
| **RED OAKS** | | | |
| Blackjack oak (*Quercus marilandica*) | 5b-9a | 30 | Widely adapted to a variety of soils. Compact, dense, smaller oak. |
| Eastern bear oak (*Q. ilicifolia*) | 5b-8a | 15 | Compact, dense, smaller oak. Drought-tolerant. |
| Northern red oak (*Q. rubra*) | 3b-9a | 75 | Adapted to average soils. One of the largest, fastest-growing, hardiest oaks. Drought- and pollution-resistant. |
| Nuttall oak (*Q. nuttallii*) | 5b-9a | 70 | Adapted to lowland sites with heavier soils. Resembles pin oak in appearance. |
| Scarlet oak (*Q. coccinea*) | 5a-9a | 65 | Adapted to upland sites with sandy soils. Resembles pin oak in appearance. |
| Shingle oak (*Q. imbricaria*) | 5a-9a | 50 | Adapted to a wide variety of soils. Easily transplanted. Slower-growing. Leaves persist year-round. |
| Shumard's red oak (*Q. Shumardii*) | 6a-9a | 75 | Adapted to poorly drained soils. Resembles northern red oak in appearance. |
| Southern red oak (*Q. falcata*) | 6b-9a | 70 | Adapted to drier soils. Resembles northern red oak in appearance. |
| Southern turkey oak (*Q. laevis*) | 8a-9b | 25 | Compact, dense, smaller oak. Drought-tolerant. |
| Water oak (*Q. nigra*) | 6b-9a | 50 | Adapted to wet, tight or well-drained soils. Resembles shingle oak in appearance. |
| Willow oak (*Q. phellos*) | 6a-9a | 50 | Adapted to wet, tight or well-drained soils. Resembles shingle oak in appearance. |
| **WHITE OAKS** | | | |
| Bur oak (*Q. macrocarpa*) | 3a-9a | 75 | Adapted to a wide variety of climates, soils and pH; very cold-hardy. Best transplanted as small tree. Picturesque branching. |
| Dwarf chestnut oak (*Q. prinoides*) | 4b-9a | 15 | Compact, smaller oak. Very tolerant of drought and alkaline soils. |
| Overcup oak (*Q. lyrata*) | 6a-9a | 60 | Adapted to poorly drained soils. Resembles bur oak in appearance. |
| Post oak (*Q. stellata*) | 6a-9a | 40 | Compact, medium-size oak. Drought-tolerant. Must be transplanted as small tree. |
| Rock chestnut oak (*Q. prinus*) | 5a-9a | 65 | Drought-tolerant. Resembles swamp chestnut oak in appearance. |
| Swamp chestnut oak (*Q. michauxii*) | 6b-9a | 75 | Adapted to poorly drained soils. Best fall color of the bur-oak types. |
| Swamp white oak (*Q. bicolor*) | 4a-8b | 60 | Adapted to poorly drained soils. One of the most easily transplanted oaks. More cold-hardy than overcup oak. |
| White oak (*Q. alba*) | 4b-9a | 75 | Picturesque branching similar to that of bur oak, with more easterly range and less tolerance of alkaline or wet soils. |
| Yellow chestnut oak (*Q. Muehlenbergii*) | 5a-8b | 65 | Tolerant of drought and alkaline soils. Resembles swamp chestnut oak in appearance. Golden fall color. |

## CULTIVARS

The red-cedar cultivars in this chart are available either from mail-order nurseries or from wholesale nurseries who accept small orders placed through local nurseries. (The sources are keyed to the nurseries listed in the box at right.) Unless otherwise noted, the cultivars grow as tree forms.

| Name | Growth habit | Comments | Sources |
|------|-------------|----------|---------|
| 'Aurea' | Conical | Variegated foliage: green and gold. | 1,4 |
| 'Burkii' | Broad columnar to conical | Foliage turns steel blue in fall and purple in winter. | 3 |
| 'Canaertii' | Columnar to conical | Dark-green, dense foliage; very numerous blue-white fruits. In Plains states, trees take on particularly dramatic forms. | 3 |
| 'Cupressifolia' | Slender conical | Fine-textured medium-green foliage. Trees of cultivar 'Hillspire' are sometimes sold under this name. | 4 |
| 'Filifera' | Broad conical | Long, slender, sweeping branchlets. | 3 |
| 'Glauca' | Columnar | Gray-green foliage; densely branching; fast growing. Also known as "silver red cedar" with several clones sold under this name. | 3 |
| 'Grey Owl' | Low, spreading shrub | Silvery-gray foliage. Same uses as widespread 'Pfitzer', which may be one parent, but branches spread more horizontally. | 2 |
| 'Pendula' | Weeping | Horizontal branches; secondary branches and branchlets hang downward. | 1,4 |
| 'Silver Spreader' | Low, spreading shrub | Similar to 'Grey Owl', but more silvery. | 5 |
| 'Skyrocket' | Very narrow columnar | Bluish-green foliage. Regularly listed as *Juniperus virginiana*, but may be a cultivar of a closely allied species, *J. scopulorum*. | 1,2,3,5,6 |

## NURSERIES

1. **Foxborough Nursery**, 3611 Miller Rd., Street, MD 21154. Mail-order. Good cultivar list, but not all in stock. Will custom-propagate. Write for information.

2. **Girard Nurseries**, P.O. Box 428, Geneva, OH 44041. Mail-order. Catalog free.

3. **Hess Nurseries, Inc.**, P.O. Box 326, Rt. 554, Cedarville, NJ 08311. Wholesale. Ships newly grafted plants in 2½-in. pots. Minimum order $50; order directly or through your local nursery.

4. **Michael A. Kristick**, 155 Mockingbird Rd., Wellsville, PA 17365. Mail-order. Write for information on plant sizes, prices and shipping.

5. **Monrovia Nursery Co.**, 18331 E. Foothill Blvd., Azusa, CA 91702. Wholesale. Good collection. Ships many sizes nationwide. Order through your local nursery.

6. **Schlichenmayer's Old Farm Nursery, Inc.**, 5550 Indiana St., Golden, CO 80403. Mail-order. Price list free. Write for information on plant sizes and shipping.

---

perus scopulorum). It's so like the eastern red cedar that some authorities consider it to be a western form or ecotype, distinguished mainly by different flowers, the blue cast of its foliage and its habit of ripening seeds the second year after their formation. The range of *J. scopulorum* covers the Rocky Mountains and extends to coastal Washington and British Columbia. I don't have room to list the cultivars, but I suspect that many of them would do well in the native range of *J. virginiana*. Indeed, among cultivars listed as red cedars, several are probably *J. scopulorum* or hybrids with *J. virginiana*, for example 'Manhattan Blue' and 'Skyrocket'.

The red cedar has few afflictions, but three are worth mentioning. Bagworms in heavy outbreaks can consume enough foliage to mar and weaken trees. But you can handpick the bags for control, and effective pesticides are also available. Deer will eat red-cedar foliage, and where deer are numerous and hungry, they may strip trees as far up as they can reach. The last problem is a disease called cedar-apple rust, which produces galls on the tree but causes it no serious harm. The disease can be devastating to susceptible apple and hawthorn cultivars, however. In an area with valuable plantings of apples or hawthorns, I suggest you not introduce the red cedar.

## Varieties

There are two ways to start with red cedars: buy nursery plants, or look for specimens in the wild and propagate them. The red cedar is uncommon in the nursery trade, largely because gardeners ask for other conifers. The chart above lists ten cultivars that are available either from mail-order sources or from wholesalers who accept orders placed through a local nursery. There are roughly 20 more cultivars in the trade, but they are grown by regional wholesalers who do not ship small orders.

To my regret, there are many red-cedar cultivars I've never seen. I've found mention of some three dozen cultivars in books such as *Hortus Third, Manual of Woody Landscape Plants* by Michael A. Dirr (Stipes Publishing Co., Box 526, Champaign, IL 61820; $24.80 softcover, $31.80 hardcover, plus $2 shipping), and *Manual of Cultivated Conifers* by Gerd Krüssman (Timber Press, 9999 S.W. Wilshire, Portland, OR 97225; $65 hardcover plus $3 shipping). If you take a fancy to uncommon cultivars, be prepared for a long search. The best place to start is an enthusiasts' group, such as the American Conifer Society (write to Maxine Schwarz, Secretary, 1264 Crummell Ave., Anapolis, MD 21403). As I'm always adding new plants to the arboretum, I'd like to hear if you find an uncommon cultivar.

As much as I value cultivars, I also en-

courage you to look for desirable red cedars in the wild. Many of our cultivars originally were found that way, and I've seen so many outstanding wild trees in my travels that I'm convinced there are many more to be discovered that are equal or superior to cultivars available in the commercial trade today. You can identify the species by the small overlapping leaves in four rows and the distinctive bark, but if you want help, carry a good field guide, such as *The Audubon Society Field Guide to North American Trees, Eastern Region* (Random House, Inc., 400 Hahn Rd., Westminster, MD 21157; $15.95 postpaid).

I ought to concede here that not all seedling trees are desirable. The best are pure beauties, and the worst are among the rattiest trees in existence. The lower branches die on some young specimens. In winter, some trees turn an unappealing brown, particularly in northern and western regions of the red cedar's native range; some trees dry up in winter and their foliage dies in patches.

When you look at wild trees, keep in mind that their features, good and bad, reflect growing conditions as well as inheritance. If the tree has been shaped by conditions, you can't expect to produce similar trees by propagation. In areas with frequent high winds, trees will be dense and compact, with highly ornamental shapes resembling large bonsai specimens. Under milder conditions, clones of these trees are likely to grow into more usual shapes. Age is another consideration. Red cedars usually are narrow and columnar when young, but eventually the lower limbs shade out, and the trees develop a distinct trunk and a wide, irregular crown. Clones of an old

The eastern red cedar, *Juniperus virginiana*, is a variable species with many striking forms. The commercially available cultivar 'Canaertii' (above left) is distinguished by a pyramidal shape, spreading branches and an open structure. This planting is at Texas Tech University in Lubbock, Texas. Author Raulston keeps an eye out for desirable wild trees, and found this weeping specimen (above right) at a highway service area in North Carolina.

The red cedar can be sheared. This Texas planting is a mix of red cedar and a closely allied species of bluer color, *Juniperus scopulorum*, native to the Rocky Mountains.

Fastigate seedlings of red cedar can make extremely narrow columns. This specimen at Willowwood Arboretum in Gladstone, New Jersey, is 40 ft. tall and 4 ft. wide.

Like the widely grown 'Pfitzer' juniper, which may be one of its parents, 'Grey Owl' makes a low spreading shrub. It is a commonly available cultivar.

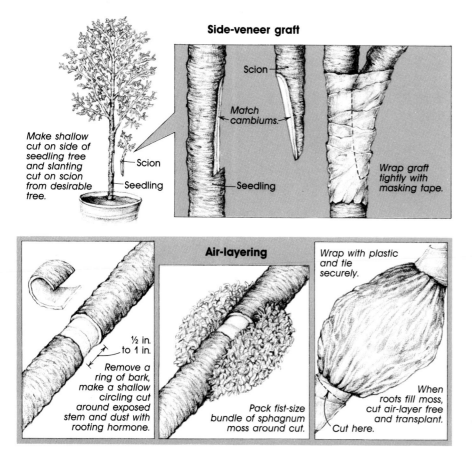

**Side-veneer graft**

Make shallow cut on side of seedling tree and slanting cut on scion from desirable tree.

Scion

Seedling

Scion

Match cambiums.

Seedling

Wrap graft tightly with masking tape.

**Air-layering**

½ in. to 1 in.

Remove a ring of bark, make a shallow circling cut around exposed stem and dust with rooting hormone.

Pack fist-size bundle of sphagnum moss around cut.

Wrap with plastic and tie securely.

When roots fill moss, cut air-layer free and transplant. Cut here.

picturesque tree will not grow in the same shape. In some cases, for example a tree loaded with berries, the only way to separate the effects of inheritance and environment is to propagate new plants and wait. The tree may be naturally fruitful, or the heavy crop may be due to kind weather. Still, you can at least be sure that the tree has fruiting potential. In other cases, a distinctive feature is inherited. Two examples of this are weeping branches and variegated foliage.

Before you decide that a particular tree is worth propagating, it would be wise to see how it looks during the winter. As a rule, I suggest that you look at a population when the trees are at their worst, and pick the good ones. Naturally, when you find a desirable tree, you should ask permission before you take cuttings.

### Growing your own

While there are several ways to propagate the red cedar, I'll focus on grafting and air-layering. Both are practical techniques for gardeners, offer fair to good prospects for success, and produce clones of the parent plant. Red cedars are easy to grow from seed, but the seedlings are not true, and vary considerably in appearance. The red cedar can also be propagated from cuttings, but not readily.

Nurseries graft on red-cedar seedlings or rooted cuttings of *J. scopulorum* 'Skyrocket', which are inexpensive because this cultivar roots readily from cuttings. The understock plants are brought into greenhouses in winter to break dormancy. The next step is to graft dormant scions on them, using a side-veneer graft wrapped with budding rubber or plastic tape to hold the union together. While the graft takes, the plants are held in high-humidity chambers or in shade to prevent moisture loss, at temperatures of 50° to 70°F to encourage rapid cell division and healing.

You should be able to adapt nursery techniques to your home resources. Start with a potted seedling. You can grow one from seed, buy it at a nursery or transplant it from the wild. In January or February, bring the pot indoors to a sunny windowsill. When new leaves begin to appear, the cambium is growing actively and is ready to accept a graft. For the scion, cut a symmetrically shaped, more or less upright branchlet or branch from the tree you want to propagate. It should have roughly the same diameter as your potted seedling does. Wrap it with a damp paper towel and put it in a plastic bag for the trip home. (If necessary, cuttings can be held several weeks in a refrigerator before they're grafted.) For the graft, take a long, shallow, vertical slice from the potted seedling near its base, and make a slanting cut of the same length and width across the base of the scion. Place the scion against the seedling, match the two cuts, and tightly fasten

the two cambium surfaces together by spiraling masking tape from top to bottom around the union. Since conifer grafts generally heal slowly, and since the red cedar can rapidly lose water and dry out, it is very important to keep conditions moist. Enclose the pot in a clear plastic bag to maintain high humidity, then set it in the indirect light of a north window to allow the union to heal. When new leaves appear on the scion, gradually cut back the seedling above the graft.

Layering is probably the surest way for a gardener to propagate the red cedar. With this technique, you prompt a branch to develop roots while it remains on the tree. The parent plant provides moisture and food while the roots grow, even if they take months to reach a useful size. Keep in mind that air-layering is suitable only for trees you can return to easily. If you find a desirable tree in another state, air-layering won't help. Take a cutting to graft instead.

To make an air-layer, select a well-shaped terminal or branchlet 6 in. to 8 in. long, remove a ring of bark about 1 in. long from the stem, and make a shallow circling cut around the stem. (Don't cut so deeply that the branchlet will snap in a windstorm.) Treat the wound with rooting hormone, and wrap a 2-in.- to 4-in.-dia. ball of moist sphagnum moss around the wound. Then tie a sheet of polyethylene film around the moss to hold it in place and to retain moisture. Secure the ends with twist-ties or tape. If the air-layer is in the sun, use white plastic, paint the plastic white or wrap it in reflective foil to prevent overheating. Check periodically for root development. When the air-layer has a good mass of roots, usually in one to four months, cut it from the tree. Harden it off and transplant it as you would any woody plant.

**I've been heartened lately** to see that red cedars are becoming prized in North Carolina. The public and landscape professionals are starting to appreciate their picturesque look, and landscapers are using tree spades to transplant specimens that are unwanted or expendable on their present sites (such as developments and old pastures). This practice could be adopted elsewhere. The trees endure transplanting with few losses. Here, the buyers often are overseers of commercial office parks and city landscapes, but there's no reason why gardeners couldn't do the same. □

*J.C. Raulston's garden is the North Carolina State University Arboretum in Raleigh, North Carolina. He writes an informative newsletter for Friends of the Arboretum. Annual membership is $15; the address is NCSU Arboretum, Dept. of Horticultural Science, Box 7609, NCSU, Raleigh, NC 27695.*

Illustrations: Laura B. Goodwin

# Dwarf Conifers

## Compact evergreens in a wealth of shapes and colors

by Robert Fincham

In 1974, I traded a fern fossil for four unusual conifers and discovered a world of plants that has been my passion ever since. As a high school science teacher, I knew only that conifers were cone-bearing trees with needle-like leaves. But I soon learned that nurserymen and collectors were growing a wide variety of conifer cultivars—trees with gold, blue or multicolored foliage, trees in the shapes of columns or globes, trees with drooping branches, trees that crawled along the ground. Most exciting of all, I discovered the dwarf conifers—slow-growing, diminutive trees that offered all the colors and shapes of their full-sized parents but needed only one-tenth the room. Because they remain naturally small without pruning, dwarf conifers are suited to sites that normal conifers outgrow—along a house foundation, beside a patio or in a mixed planting with shrubs and perennials, for example. These plants also enliven the garden with year-round color, distinctive foliage and the surprise of their miniature stature.

I became a collector of dwarf conifers and eventually a nurseryman, and along the way I learned many things, including how to find and use good cultivars. I started a small retail business, in part because I'd found that when a rare plant died, a replacement for it was often impossible to find. Now there are a number of other nurseries specializing in dwarf conifers, making it relatively easy for newcomers to get started with these plants. (For a list of nurseries, see Resources on p. 93.

Dwarf conifers enliven the garden with a rich variety of colors and shapes while demanding far less space than normal-size evergreens. Here, a 2-ft. tall statue nestles among several dwarf and compact conifers, including a foot-high white pine, just visible at lower left, a conical blue spruce on the right, and a 6-ft. tall spruce in the back that glows with yellow-colored new growth.

The blue needles and spiky texture of 'Globosa', a dwarf cultivar of the Colorado blue spruce, contrast strikingly with a clump of fountain grass. Dwarf conifers are suited to the perennial border where they add novel colors and textures, provide winter interest and rarely infringe on their neighbors.

A mounding dwarf white pine, at 3 ft. tall, barely overtops a clump of Shasta daisies. The pine's dense needles are distinctive.

## Dwarf conifer cultivars

*Here is a selection of desirable dwarf conifer cultivars, all available from specialty nurseries.*

**Miniatures,** attaining a size of less than 3 ft. in 20 years.

**Cypresses,** Hinoki cypress, *Chamaecyparis obtusa*; 'Golden Sprite' (gold); Sawara cypress, *C. pisifera* 'Tsukumo'

**Spruces,** Norway spruce, *Picea abies* 'Little Gem'; *P. mariana* 'Nana'

**Mountain pine,** *Pinus mugo* 'Mitsch Mini'

**Canada hemlock,** *Tsuga canadensis* 'Minuta'

**Globes,** somewhat spherical shape, attaining a diameter of 6 ft. in 20 years.

**Firs,** balsam fir, *Abies balsamea* 'Nana'; alpine fir, *A. lasiocarpa* 'Green Globe'

**Himalayan cedar,** *Cedrus deodara* 'Hollandia'

**Sawara cypress,** *Chamaecyparis pisifera* 'Gold Dust' (gold variegated)

**Japanese cedar,** *Cryptomeria japonica* 'Vilmoriniana'

**Common juniper,** *Juniperus communis* 'Berkshire'

**Spruces,** Norway spruce, *Picea abies* 'Pumila Nigra'; white spruce, *P. glauca* 'Little Globe'; Oriental spruce, *P. orientalis* 'Barnes'; Colorado blue spruce, *P. pungens* 'St. Mary' (blue)

**Pines,** scrub pine, *Pinus banksiana* 'Manomet'; mountain pine, *P. mugo* 'Sherwood Compact'; white pine, *P. strobus* 'Horsford', 'Merrimack', 'Sea Urchin'; Scots pine, *P. sylvestris* 'Beuvronensis'; Japanese black pine, *P. thunbergiana* 'Banshoho'

**Douglas fir,** *Pseudotsuga menziesii* 'Pumila'

**English yew,** *Taxus baccata* 'Fowle's Dwarf'

**American arborvitae,** *Thuja occidentalis* 'Hetz Midget'; 'Tiny Tim'

**Hiba arborvitae** *Thujopsis dolobrata* 'Nana'

**Canada hemlock,** *Tsuga canadensis* 'Rugg's Washington Dwarf'

**Uprights,** conical shape, attaining a height of 6 ft. in 20 years.

**White fir,** *Abies concolor* 'Compacta' (blue)

**Hinoki cypress,** *Chamaecyparis obtusa* 'Hage', 'Nana', 'Nana Lutea' (gold), 'Spiralis'

**Japanese white pine,** *Pinus parviflora* 'Adcock's Dwarf'

**Douglas fir,** *Pseudotsuga menziesii* 'Little Jon'

**Canada hemlock,** *Tsuga canadensis* 'Everitt's Golden' (gold), 'Jervis', 'Lewis'

**Prostrate forms,** grow flat along the ground if not staked and will probably cover up to 15 ft. in 20 years.

**Cedar-of-Lebanon,** *Cedrus libani* 'Sargentii'

**Norway spruce,** *Picea abies* 'Frohburg'

**Scots pine,** *Pinus sylvestris* 'Hillside Creeper', 'Repens'

**Hemlocks,** Canada hemlock, *Tsuga canadensis* 'Cole's Prostrate'; *T. carolina* 'Labar's Weeping'

For a selection of reliable and attractive cultivars, see the table at left.)

## What is dwarf?

When I say *dwarf conifer*, I mean a tree that grows to a height or width of less than 6 ft. in 20 years. As you might expect, there are varying definitions of "dwarf conifer" among nurseries, collectors and horticulturists, so be sure you learn all you can about a cultivar before you buy it. Some cultivars are misidentified as dwarfs and soon get too large for their site. Others are "compact," not dwarf. For example, the blue spruce cultivar 'R.H. Montgomery' and the false cypress cultivar 'Nana Gracilis', though often sold as dwarf conifers, are actually larger than dwarfs, though still far smaller than normal trees. At the other extreme are miniatures, trees that grow less than 3 ft. in 20 years. They are best suited to rock gardens and similar displays of small plants.

Dwarf conifers are mutations. They appear either as slow-growing seedlings of normal trees or as mysteriously slow-growing shoots called witches'-brooms on otherwise-normal trees. (For more about witches'-brooms, see p. 92.) Most of the cultivars available today were found as uncommonly small trees in nursery seed beds, Christmas tree plantations or the wild. They arise infrequently and are usually found by happenstance, though some enthusiasts do search for them. My friend Layne Ziegenfuss would spend days walking through Christmas tree plantations looking for freaks, and he found several excellent cultivars, among them *Pinus sylvestris* 'Hillside Creeper'. Trees stunted by growing conditions are not dwarfs. Bonsai trees, for example, kept small by regular pruning of their branches and roots, would grow to normal size in the wild, and alpine trees, slowed by the harsh climate at high elevations, would resume normal growth if moved to lower altitudes.

To be identical to the original plant, a dwarf cultivar must be propagated by cuttings or by grafting. Cuttings are snippets of the original tree, kept under moist, warm conditions until they strike roots. Grafts consist of a scion (a shoot from the original tree) fitted to a seedling of the same or a compatible species. The two parts knit together, and the scion grows into a dwarf tree. Sometimes, however, the root system forces the scion to grow faster than

Nearly 40 years old but barely 3 ft. tall, this tree of the false cypress cultivar 'Nana Lutea', with dense, gold foliage and a craggy shape, makes a striking specimen in the rock garden. In a foundation planting, it would never outgrow its place.

All parts of a dwarf conifer are small. The needles of this dwarf white pine are 2 in. long, shorter by at least half than the needles of a normal white pine. Branches are shorter and closer together, too, as the growing points in this photo show.

Grafted high on a straight trunk and growing naturally in a blue globe, the juniper cultivar 'Blue Star' will not outgrow its site at the foot of a masonry wall. Dwarf conifers are ideal foundation plants because they will not grow up against the house or into the eaves.

expected, most frequently a problem in grafts of hemlock, spruce or false cypress. Rooted cuttings are safer, but many species will not root and must be grafted. Nurseries that specialize in dwarf conifers understand the pitfalls of propagation and provide young trees that are truly dwarf.

A dwarf conifer is named only if propagated plants grow like the original plant. Observation takes years, since some seemingly dwarf trees grow slowly when young and then accelerate as they mature. When a friend of mine discovered a very slow-growing native hemlock (*Tsuga canadensis*) with

white needles on its branch tips, he waited ten years to name it 'Mt. Hood'.

## Landscape merits

The chief attraction of conifers is their needle-like, evergreen foliage, which provides interest year-round and is a nice contrast to the broad leaves of

# Witches'-brooms yield new dwarf conifers
by Sidney Waxman

Where do new dwarf conifers come from? While most are chance seedlings found by observant horticulturists, the rest come from an intriguing source: witches'-brooms, dense growths of closely spaced leaves and branches that arise from mutated buds on full-size trees. I collect their seeds and grow new dwarf conifers for the garden.

The most exciting aspect of growing seedlings is their variability. From plant to plant, everything varies: needle length and color, branching habit, shape and size. The plants can be miniature, dwarf or intermediate in size; columnar, mounded, spreading or weeping in form; and blue-green, green, yellow or gold in color. The seeds of witches'-brooms are a trove of possibilities for the garden.

Collecting seeds from witches'-brooms is tricky business. Brooms tend to appear near the tops of trees or at the ends of branches. During my first ten years of collecting, I climbed trees and sometimes took risks because so few brooms had cones. Finally, I found myself at the top of a terribly thin Eastern larch in an open

field in Bar Harbor, Maine. Clinging to the tree while it swayed dangerously in a strong wind, I decided that there must be a safer way to collect seeds.

Atop the white pine in the distance, a single mutated bud has produced the characteristically dense growth of a witches'-broom. Collecting the cones of this broom was risky but worthwhile: seedlings of witches'-brooms often produce garden-worthy dwarf conifers.

For a while, I collected cones with a pole pruner, adding sections to the handle so I could reach brooms as high as 30 ft. Unfortunately, I often spotted cones on brooms near the tops of trees 35 ft. to 75 ft. high. I tried shooting cones down. Though I found that I could bring down cone-bearing twigs by using a .22-caliber rifle with a gunsight, my accuracy was not always reliable. On the first trip, I did well until I shot at a broom that was very high up. After several hundred rounds, I accomplished only the destruction of the broom. On the return trip through Massachusetts, which had a mandatory jail sentence for possession of a gun, I worried about having to explain to a state trooper just what I was doing. Wiser now, I hire professional tree workers to collect the cones of witches'-brooms.

Today, the Horticulture Research Nursery at the University of Connecticut, where I grow the seeds of witches'-brooms, boasts thousands of dwarf conifers. The collection includes seedlings of Norway spruce, Canada hemlock, Eastern larch and six pine species—white, red, Scots, pitch, Jack and Japanese red.

I have named and introduced 23 new dwarf conifer cultivars, resisting the temptation to name dozens more. Several white pine cultivars are available, including 'Sea Urchin', 'Soft Touch', 'Blue Shag', 'Blue Jay' and 'Golden Candles', as well as the Eastern larch cultivar 'Newport Beauty'. In the future, cultivars from Eastern larch, white pine, Canada hemlock and Japanese red pine will be available as well. Clearly the seedlings of witches'-brooms are an excellent source of choice plants. We are just beginning to appreciate and exploit their variability.

Grown and observed for years by the author, seedlings of witches'-brooms fill nursery beds with varying shapes, sizes and colors.

Sidney Waxman is a professor of plant science at the University of Connecticut, Storrs, Connecticut.

most woody plants. Many gardeners think first of flowers when landscaping and overlook foliage, but a garden focused on flowers can look almost too showy in spring and summer and drab in the winter. Adding conifers to a landscape tempers the intensity of spring and summer flowers and provides welcome color in the winter garden. Using conifers of different colors—blue, gold, pale green, variegated—heightens the trees' contribution to the landscape.

Dwarf conifers have their place in the large garden, and they are essential space savers in the small garden. Their variety of shapes—columns, mounds, fountains, groundcovers—suits them for planting as specimens, accents and foundation plants. In foundation plantings, combine them with other suitably sized shrubs such as azaleas, dwarf rhododendrons or dwarf viburnums. Keep the plants 3 ft. to 5 ft. away from the house and put taller plants at the house corners and near the doors. In borders and island beds, mix dwarf conifers with perennials and annuals, or use them as trees in miniature rock garden landscapes. Planted near a fence, dwarf conifers will subdue its harsh horizontal and vertical lines. The plants will stay in scale with their site for many years and, unlike their normal parents, will not crowd out their neighbors or stunt them with extensive shade.

When combining dwarf conifers with other plants, you can use varying shapes and colors: the blue spruce *Picea pungens* 'St. Mary' is a small, blue mound; the white pine *Pinus strobus* 'Horsford' makes a light green ball; the false cypress *Chamaecyparis obtusa* 'Hage' grows into a dark green cone; and another false cypress, 'Nana Lutea', also makes a cone, but a bright gold one. Suppose one corner of your garden lies in the shade of a small, flowering tree. Here, you can plant shade-tolerant dwarf hemlocks mixed with azaleas and rhododendrons for a backdrop. The ground-hugging hemlock cultivar *Tsuga canadensis* 'Cole's Prostrate' can serve as a ground cover in the heavier shade while the low-mounding cultivar *T. canadensis* 'Jeddeloh' can grow in lighter shade.

When used in a rock garden, dwarf conifers should be scattered throughout the planting. Upright cultivars suggest trees, while prostrate ones, cascading over and between rocks, add character. Choose plants suited to the size of the garden. If the rock garden is small, use miniatures. For a larger garden, you may be able to use even compact forms instead of true dwarfs. Pruning can create a windswept look. For example, *Picea abies* 'Little Gem' is a Norway spruce that develops into a small, dense bun. By pruning much of the foliage and many of the branches, you can shape it to resemble a miniature spruce tree.

Properly chosen dwarf conifers are low-maintenance plants. I have noticed a common misconception about dwarf conifers: that they need pruning to stay dwarf. This unfortunate belief has developed among some gardeners because trees they purchased as dwarf conifers turned out not to be dwarf at all. While dwarf conifers never stop growing, they grow very slowly and need pruning only for shape and health—to remove poorly placed or unhealthy branches.

## Getting started

Before you shop for dwarf conifers, study the cultivars available. There are several good books about conifers that include information about dwarf forms (see Resources at left). Visiting conifer collections is an excellent way to learn more. Search out people with unusual plants. A visit to your local arboretum can provide a few names, and the arboretum may also have its own collection of dwarf conifers.

Dwarf conifers are not always easy to find at local nurseries. Garden centers tend to shy away from these plants for two basic reasons. First, dwarf conifers take a long time to raise in the nursery, so they are expensive, and it's difficult to sell a small plant for a high price. Second, few people, even in garden centers, are knowledgeable about dwarf conifers. But look around—there are garden centers with good dwarf conifer selections.

The most convenient way to acquire dwarf conifers is from specialty nurseries that sell by mail. They offer the greatest selection of cultivars, including most of the rare ones. The only drawback is that plants bought through the mail, due mainly to shipping limitations, will be too small to make a show immediately. You can set them in their permanent places, or keep them in a nursery bed for a year or two before moving them into the landscape.

A landscape with dwarf conifers can provide years of pleasure with little demand on your time or energy. The initial cost of the plants may seem high, but as the years go by, the price becomes a bargain. □

*Robert Fincham is a founder and past president of The American Conifer Society, and the owner of Mitsch Nursery and Coenosium Gardens, conifer nurseries in Aurora, Oregon.*

# Index

## A

American Conifer Society, address for, 86
American Peony Society, address for, 15
American Rose Society, address for, 38
Andromeda. *See* Pieris.
*Audubon Society Field Guide to North American Trees,* source for, 86

## B

Beaubaire, Nancy, on weeping trees, 72
Beech, weeping *(Fagus sylvatica* 'Tortuosa'), growing, 73
Black spot, control of, 47
Bogusch, Rick, on viburnums, 17-21
Botrytis, control of, 16
Buckeyes *(Aesculus* spp.):
    bottlebrush buckeye *(A. parviflora),* 25
    California buckeye *(A. californica),* 24-25
    Ohio buckeye *(A. glabra),* 24
    planting, 25
    red buckeye *(A. pavia),* 23-24
    sources for, 24
    starting from seed, 25

## C

Cherry, weeping *(Prunus subhirtella),* growing, 68, 69
Chlorosis, prevention of, 29
*Classic Roses* (Beales), source for, 38
*Combined Rose List* (Dobson), source for, 46
*Companion to Roses, The* (Fisher), source for, 38
Conifers, dwarf:
    book on, 93
    cultivars of, 90
    discussed, 89, 91
    landscaping with, 92-93
    new cultivars from witches'-brooms, 92
    society for, 93
    sources for, 93
Crabapples *(Malus* spp.):
    care of, 60
    disease-resistant varieties of, 57, 59, 60
    society for, 60

## D

De Blasi, Anthony, on tree peonies, 12-16
Druitt, Liz, on old roses for hot climates, 35
Dunn, Dave, on old roses, 30-35

## F

Fertilizers:
    slow-release, 46
    soluble, 47
    trace-element, 47
Fincham, Robert, on dwarf conifers, 89-93
Fringe trees *(Chionanthus* spp.):
    Chinese *(C. retusus),* 67
    old-man's-beard *(C. virginicus),* 66-67
    pygmy *(C. pygmaea),* 67
    sources for, 67

## G

Galle, Fred C., on hollies, 74-79
Green, Thomas L., on outstanding crabapples, 56-60

## H

Hemlock, Canadian *(Tsuga canadensis):*
    book on, 69
    Sargent's weeping *(T. canadensis* f. *pendula),* 69-70
Heritage Rose Foundation, address for, 38
Heritage Roses Group, address for, 38
*History of the Rose, The* (Shepherd), source for, 38
Holly *(Ilex* spp.):
    choosing species and cultivars, 76-77
    deciduous types, 78-79
    evergreen types, 74-79
    how to get berries, 77
    landscape uses of, 77
    list of cultivars, 77
    planting and caring for, 78-79
    range of, 75, 77
    society for, 78
    sources for, 78
Holly Society of America, address for, 78

## I

International Lilac Society, address for, 10
International Ornamental Crabapple Society, address for, 60

## K

Katsura, weeping *(Cercidiphyllum* spp.), growing, 70-72

## L

Lacebugs, control of, 29
Landscaping:
    with dwarf conifers, 92-93
    with holly, 77
    with oak trees, 81-84
    with old roses, 39-41
    with pieris, 27
    with red cedar, 85
Lilacs *(Syringa* spp.):
    book on, 10
    in the garden, 9
    growing, 10-11
    recommended varieties, 10
    society for, 10
    sources for, 10
*Lilacs—The Genus Syringa* (Fiala), source for, 10
Lowe, Mike, on miniature roses, 42-47
Lowman, Larry P., on native buckeyes, 22-25

## M

Magnolias, hardy:
    blooming time and blossoms, 51-52
    culture, 54
    evergreen magnolias, 53
    hardiness of and microclimates for, 54
    hybrid magnolias, 53-54
    for large gardens, 52
    planting and transplanting, 54
    pruning, 54
    for small gardens, 52-52
    society for, 54
    sources for, 54
    varieties, 52-54
Magnolia Society, address for, 54
*Manual of Cultivated Conifers* (Krüssman), source for, 86
*Manual of Woody Landscape Plants* (Dirr), source for, 86
Mildew, control of, 47
*Modern Roses 9* (American Rose Society), source for, 38

## N

Nicholson, Rob:
    on fringe trees, 66-67
    on weeping trees, 68-73

## O

Oaks *(Quercus* spp.):
    books on, 84
    for landscape, 83
    range of, 80-81
    red oaks, 81
    sources for, 84
    white oaks, 81-84

## P

Parrotia, weeping (*Parrotia pendula* 'Persica'), growing, 72
Peonies, tree (*Paeonia suffruticosa* or *lutea*):
  cultivars of, 14-15
  described, 12-14
  growing, 14, 16
  pests and diseases of, 16
  society for, 15
  sources for, 15
Pieris:
  growing, 29
  landscape uses of, 27
  pests and diseases of, 29
  *P. floribunda*, 28
  *P. japonica*, 27-28
  sources for, 29
Pruning:
  magnolias, 54
  roses, 34, 47, 49

## R

Raulston, J.C.:
  on redbuds, 61-65
  on red cedar, 85-88
Ray, Martin, on *Rosa rubrifolia*, 48-49
Redbuds (*Cercis* spp.):
  chain-flowered redbud (*C. racemosa*), 65
  Chinese redbud (*C. chinensis*), 65
  eastern redbud (*C. canadensis*), 62-63
  Mediterranean redbud (*C. siliquastrum*), 65
  Mexican redbud (*C. mexicana*), 64
  sources for, 65
  starting from seed, 62
  Texas redbud (*C. reniformis*), 63-64
  western redbud (*C. occidentalis*), 64-65
Red cedar (*Juniperus virginiana*):
  cultivars of, 86
  in the landscape, 85-86
  propagating, 88
  qualities of, 85-88
  sources for, 86
*Rosa rubrifolia*:
  landscaping with, 48
  maintaining, 48-49
  pruning, 49
  sources for, 49

Roses (*Rosa* spp.):
  miniature, 42-47
    in the garden, 43-44
    pests and diseases of, 47
    planting, 44, 46
    pruning, 47
    sources for, 46
    varieties of, 46
  old, 30-35, 36-41
    books on, 38
    Dowager Queen Award for, 32
    groups, 31
    hardy in warm climates, 35
    identifying, 38
    landscaping with, 39-41
    maintaining, 33-34
    pests and diseases of, 34, 36
    planting, soil preparation for, 32-33
    propagating, 36, 41
    pruning of, 34
    societies for, 34, 38
    sources for, 34, 38
    spraying, 34
    varieties of, 32
  *See also Rosa rubrifolia.*
Ryniec, Daniel K., on lilacs, 8-11

## S

Schmidt, Melvin L., on hardy magnolias, 50-55
Shoup, Michael, Jr., on old roses, 36-41
Spider mites, control of, 47
Sternberg, Guy, on growing oak trees, 80-84

## T

Trees:
  oak, 80-84
  weeping, 68-73
    landscape uses of, 69
    sources for, 72
  *See also* Crabapples. Fringe trees. Magnolias, hardy. Redbuds. Red cedar.

## V

Van Etten, Joyce, on *Pieris*, 26-29
Viburnums (*Viburnum* spp.):
  choosing, 18-19
  growing, 20
  varieties of, 19-20, 21

## W

Waxman, Sidney, on collecting witches'-brooms, 92
Witches'-brooms, new dwarf conifers from, 92

The 18 articles in this book originally appeared in *Fine Gardening* magazine. The date of first publication, issue number and page numbers for each article are given below.

| | | |
|---|---|---|
| 8 | Lilacs | May 1992 (25:66-69) |
| 12 | Tree Peonies | July 1990 (14:22-26) |
| 17 | Viburnums | July 1992 (26:65-69) |
| 22 | Buckeyes | September 1991 (21:24-27) |
| 26 | In Praise of Pieris | March 1992 (24:60-63) |
| 30 | Old Roses for the Small Garden | January 1991 (17:24-29) |
| 36 | Old Roses | November 1988 (4:58-63) |
| 42 | Miniature Roses | March 1989 (6:18-23) |
| 48 | Rosa Rubrifolia | November 1991 (22:54-55) |
| 50 | Hardy Magnolias | March 1991 (18:26-31) |
| 56 | Outstanding Crabapples | March 1992 (24:26-30) |
| 61 | Redbuds | May 1991 (19:71-75) |
| 66 | Fringe Trees | July 1992 (26:52-53) |
| 68 | Weeping Trees | March 1990 (12:40-45) |
| 74 | Hollies | September 1991 (21:68-73) |
| 80 | The Mighty Oaks | November 1990 (16:65-69) |
| 85 | Eastern Red Cedar | January 1989 (5:53-56) |
| 89 | Dwarf Conifers | January 1992 (23:47-51) |

# If you enjoyed this book, you're going to love our magazine.

A year's subscription to *Fine Gardening* brings you the kind of hands-on information you found in this book, and much more. In issue after issue—six times a year—you'll find articles on nurturing specific plants, landscape design, fundamentals and building structures. Expert gardeners will share their knowledge and techniques with you. They will show you how to apply their knowledge in your own backyard. Filled with detailed illustrations and full-color photographs, *Fine Gardening* will inspire you to create and realize your dream garden!

To subscribe, just fill out one of the attached subscription cards or call us at 1-203-426-8171. And as always, your satisfaction is guaranteed, or we'll give you your money back.

**Taunton**
BOOKS & VIDEOS
*for fellow enthusiasts*

The Taunton Press 63 S. Main Street, P.O. Box 5506, Newtown, CT 06470-5506

# FINE GARDENING

Use this card to subscribe to *Fine Gardening* or to request information about other Taunton Press magazines, books and videos.

☐ 1 year (6 issues) $26
$32 outside the U.S.

☐ 2 years (12 issues) $42
$52 outside the U.S.

(U.S. funds, please. Canadian residents: GST included)

Name _____
Address _____
City _____
State _____ Zip _____

☐ My payment is enclosed.     ☐ Please bill me.
☐ Please send me information about other Taunton Press magazines, books and videos.

I'm interested in:
1 ☐ sewing
2 ☐ home building
3 ☐ woodworking
4 ☐ gardening
5 ☐ other                                    BFG1

---

# FINE GARDENING

Use this card to subscribe to *Fine Gardening* or to request information about other Taunton Press magazines, books and videos.

☐ 1 year (6 issues) $26
$32 outside the U.S.

☐ 2 years (12 issues) $42
$52 outside the U.S.

(U.S. funds, please. Canadian residents: GST included)

Name _____
Address _____
City _____
State _____ Zip _____

☐ My payment is enclosed.     ☐ Please bill me.
☐ Please send me information about other Taunton Press magazines, books and videos.

I'm interested in:
1 ☐ sewing
2 ☐ home building
3 ☐ woodworking
4 ☐ gardening
5 ☐ other                                    BFG1

**Taunton**
M A G A Z I N E S
*for fellow enthusiasts*

# BUSINESS REPLY MAIL
FIRST CLASS MAIL   PERMIT NO.19   NEWTOWN CT

POSTAGE WILL BE PAID BY ADDRESSEE

THE TAUNTON PRESS
63 SOUTH MAIN STREET
PO BOX 5506
NEWTOWN CT 06470-9955

---

**Taunton**
M A G A Z I N E S
*for fellow enthusiasts*

# BUSINESS REPLY MAIL
FIRST CLASS MAIL   PERMIT NO.19   NEWTOWN CT

POSTAGE WILL BE PAID BY ADDRESSEE

THE TAUNTON PRESS
63 SOUTH MAIN STREET
PO BOX 5506
NEWTOWN CT 06470-9955